RES PUBLICA

Tang Chun-I Lecture Series

The Tang Chun-I Lecture Series is based on lectures and seminars delivered by distinguished scholars who are holding the Tang Chun-I Visiting Professorship at The Chinese University of Hong Kong. This professorship was initiated in 2003 by the Department of Philosophy, The Chinese University of Hong Kong, in memory of the late Professor Tang Chun-I (1909–1978), a major figure in twentieth-century Chinese philosophy and the first Chair Professor of the Department of Philosophy.

A volume in the SUNY series in Contemporary Continental Philosophy

Dennis J. Schmidt, editor

RES PUBLICA

Plato's *Republic* in Classical German Philosophy

Günter Zöller

The Tang Chun-I Lecture for 2012

State University of New York Press

The Chinese University Press

ISBN: The Chinese University Press 978-962-996-645-4
ISBN: State University of New York Press 978-1-4384-5881-6

Published for North America by:
State University of New York Press
Albany, New York
www.sunypress.edu

Published for the rest of the world by:
The Chinese University Press
The Chinese University of Hong Kong
Sha Tin, N.T., Hong Kong
Fax: +852 2603 7355
E-mail: cup@cuhk.edu.hk
Website: www.chineseupress.com

Printed in Hong Kong

Library of Congress Cataloging-in-Publication Data
Günter Zöller, 1954–
Plato's Republic in Classical German Philosophy / Günter Zöller
(SUNY series in Contemporary Continental Philosophy)
ISBN 978-1-4384-5881-6 (hardcover: alk. Paper)

Library of Congress Control Number: 2014959870

10 9 8 7 6 5 4 3 2 1

Uxori

Contents

Preface

This book arose from the public lecture and the faculty seminar I delivered as the seventeenth holder of the Tang Chun-I Visiting Professorship in Philosophy at The Chinese University of Hong Kong in the fall of 2012.

For their published presentation, the lecture's treatment of Kant's Plato and the seminar's presentation of Hegel's Plato were supplemented by a portrayal of Fichte's Plato—all three readings carried out with a focus on the unifying theme of Plato's *Republic* as a source of intellectual inspiration as much as an object of critical engagement in classical German philosophy.

The book's three core chapters, with their progression from the ideal republic in Kant through the real republic in Hegel to the people's republic in Fichte, are complemented by an introduction on the relationship of Plato's political philosophy, as contained in the *Republic*, to the republican legacy in Western political thought and by an appendix presenting my English translation, along with the German original, of a short text by Fichte titled "Plato Republic," dating from around 1807, which only recently has been published for the first time. Fichte's brief commentary on the first few books of the *Republic* serves to document his particular concern with Plato's primary political text.

The point of the proposed parallels between Plato and the neo-Platonism of Kant, Fichte and Hegel is not a historical study of influence but a philosophical consideration of import. By effectuating an encounter between an ancient thinker and his modern descendants, a confluence of currents and a convergence of movements is to be brought about that provides the ancient past with a modern mirror and the modern positions with an ancient context. Such an artificial mutual encounter is apt to shed light, or at least generate some heat, in an area where the differences between old and new ways of thinking and doing are especially apparent—the political sphere and the philosophical reflection on it.

The larger context of research and teaching out of which the present book grew includes the graduate seminar I gave at The Chinese University under the auspices of the Tang Chun-I Visiting Professorship in October 2012, titled "Republics Old and New. Political Freedom in Classical Greek and Modern European Philosophy," and a similar seminar I taught to graduate students from McGill University, Université de Montréal and Concordia University at McGill University in November 2012. The chief concerns of both courses were the continuities and discontinuities between ancient and modern thinking about the commonwealth (*res publica*) and the specifically different relationship between the human individual and the political community in the Greek city-state and in the modern sovereign territorial state.

I would like to thank the Department of Philosophy of The Chinese University of Hong Kong for inviting me to serve as the 17th Tang Chun-I Visiting Professor. In particular, I would like to express my gratitude and appreciation to the colleagues and students in the Department for their interest in my work and their eagerness to discuss my views. Special thanks go to my friend and colleague in the Department Tze-wan Kwan for his gracious hospitality during my stay.

The exceptional cultural, economic and political status of Hong Kong, along with the New Territories, as a Special Administrative Region (SAR) was as much on my mind in lecturing about republics old and new at The Chinese University of Hong Kong, as was the unique historical and current situation of Montreal, along with that of the province of Quebec, when I developed the work first presented in Hong Kong as one of my research projects under the auspices of the John G. Diefenbaker Award of the Canadian Council for the Arts (2012–13). For the academic hospitality I received during my year in Canada, I wish to thank the Department of Philosophy at McGill University, especially my host George di Giovanni.

I was able to finish work on this book in another extraordinary city, Venice, which can lay claim to the longest duration of republican self-governance, spanning more than a thousand years. A further republican setting of this and my other work has been the global republic of letters constituted by my doctoral students present and past, from sixteen countries on five continents, who have helped me in widening my intellectual and cultural horizons and placing my own philosophical positions in proper perspective.

Venice
January 2013

Professor Günter Zöller
(Photograph by Jeff Li)

Front row from left: Professor Kwan Tze-wan, Professor Günter Zöller, Professor Wong Kai-yee. Back row from left: Professor Liu Xiaogan, Professor Lau Chong-fuk, Professor Li Hon-lam, Professor Wang Qingjie, Professor Cheng Chung-yi, Dr. Lo Kit-hung, Professor Cheung Kam-ching Leo, Professor Saulius Geniusas. (Photograph by Jeff Li)

Note on Citations

In keeping with the condensed and comparative scope of the present study, scholarly references are largely limited to providing bibliographical documentation.

The primary texts by Kant, Fichte and Hegel are cited according to the authoritative modern editions of their works, as detailed in the bibliography, supplemented by references to modern English translations, where available. References to other literature are, for the most, limited to recent English-language works.

As customary, Kant's *Critique of Pure Reason* (Kant 1781/1787) is cited by the original pagination of the first and second editions, indicated as "A" and "B," respectively, which is recorded in modern editions and translations of the work.

1

The Polity: Plato and the Republican Legacy

"[E]xtra rempublicam nulla salus."[1]

Plato's "ten books on the constitution of the citizen state"—so the *Republic*'s ancient descriptive title—is one of the founding texts of Western political philosophy. Together with Aristotle's "treatises on matters political"—this the descriptive title of what came to be known as *The Politics*—it has served as the source of inspiration and the subject of interpretation, but also as the target of emendation and the object of irritation for much subsequent thinking about the forms and norms of that most characteristically, if not exclusively, human of societies, alternatively labeled "political community" (*koinonia politike*), "commonwealth" (*res publica*), "civil society" (*societas civilis*) and "state" (*status*).

Still the placement of Plato's masterly middle dialogue in the specific tradition of republican political thought might seem inappropriate and even counterindicated, given that tradition's essential emphasis on freedom within and without as the hallmark of the proper form of political life. By contrast, Plato in his published political thinking seems more focused and intent on psychic and societal order, and this apparently at the expense of freedom or "liberty." In the context of the twentieth century's horrific experience with totalitarian ideologies on both extremes of the political spectrum, Plato's perceived illiberalism has even brought upon him the charge of being an "enemy of the open society" and of ignoring and even opposing the political goal of freedom.[2]

Moreover, the terminology and conceptuality of republican political thought goes back not to Plato—or any Greek political theory and practice, for that matter—but to Roman political history and its discursive reflection in philosophy, historiography and oratory.[3] The very name "republic" along with its equivalents in other languages such as *république* and *reppublica*, employed in modern translations of the Greek title term for Plato's work (*Politeia*), utilizes the Latin designation for the Roman body politic, *res publica*, literally meaning "public matter" or "public affair."

Still, the superimposition of Roman republican theory and practice on Plato's political thinking about the ideal state within the specifically Greek context of the city-state (*polis*) and its constitution (*politeia*) is not without some cause and merit. The emphasis that the classical Roman Republic placed or claimed to place on civic life, focusing on its citizens' public obligations—termed *officia* and meaning "offices" as much as "duties"—and extolling the public at the expense of the private, effectively links Roman republicanism backward to Plato's republic and its philosophically justified primacy of the political over the personal, the communal over the individual and the universal over the particular.

From a perspective informed by Roman republican thinking and doing, Plato's republic even appears quite un-Greek in that it lacks all the features the republican Romans noticed and minded in a political life form such as that of classical Athens, marked by division, strife and change and factually as well as structurally prone to that most excessive and unstable form of political life—"democracy" or popular rule.[4] By contrast, Plato's republic, while lacking the distinctively Roman republican feature of self-rule—of political freedom from domestic as well as foreign domination—resonated with the republican *ethos* of self-control and mastery of oneself that distinguished free citizens from unfree inhabitants and from those who, while formally free, were slaves to their own uncurbed passions and unchecked desires.

But the Roman Republic—in its idealized self-interpretation to be found in the works of Cicero, Livy and Tacitus—not only shares the Platonic psychosocial ideal of self-mastery and self-control. It also follows Platonic political thinking in having the *polis*, or rather the *res publica*, governed not by individual persons ("men") but by rules of conduct ("laws") designed to remove the exercise of political power from arbitrary choice and purely personal preference. The order at which Plato's republic is aiming, which might seem detrimental to freedom, is an order borne by the twin principle of psychic and social order, namely, of ethical as well as political righteousness or "justice" (*diakaiosyne*). To be sure, the classical Roman republican take on ethico-political justice includes the framing and taming of the citizens' freedom through censorial control intent on curbing the human proclivities toward luxury and license, just as Plato's philosophical *polis* is marked by severe social strictures and extensive educational efforts imposed in the interest of having the citizens' personal and political lives be shaped by the principle of justice.

The conceptual distance between Plato's republic and actual Greek political life, together with the former's considerable alternative affinity to key elements of the Roman republican *ethos*, also shows itself in the exceptional relation of Plato's republic, as well as that of the Roman Republic, to the Greek constitutional classifications. In the *Republic* Plato does not characterize the emerging ideal city-state by resorting to the numerically informed typology of political constitutions to be found in Aristotle's *Politics* and already contained in Plato's later political dialogue on the statesman (*Politikos*), which distinguishes the rule of one (monarchy), the rule of few (aristocracy) and the rule of many (democracy).[5] Nor does the *Republic* address the cyclical turnover among the three constitutional types and their correlated degenerative forms (tyranny, oligarchy, ochlocracy).

Rather Plato juxtaposes the city-state erected in the political imagination of Socrates and his interlocutors to a comprehensive range of known constitutions that are all deemed defective in one way or another and that range from the political rule based on honor (timocracy) through the political rule of the few rich (oligarchy) and of the many poor (democracy) to despotic political rule (tyranny). Accordingly, the ideal constitution of the city-state sought in the *Republic* resembles none of the known constitutional types. The same could be said of Plato's detailed plan for the second-best city-state laid out in the *Republic*'s late companion work, *The Laws* (*Nomoi*). There is no hereditary monarchy or entrenched aristocracy nor a freely ruling wider populace to be found in either of those works. Instead there is the supreme rule of law, more internalized through comprehensive civic education in the *Republic* and more externally imposed in the *Laws*.

The Roman republican counterpart to the atypical status of Plato's republic is the former's self-understanding as a mixed constitution,[6] not in the sense of an artificial combination of heterogeneous constitutional types but as the institutional recognition of the need to contain and control the exercise of political power by means of a well-equilibrated arrangement of offices and authorities, chiefly composed of the regularly rotating kingly power of the supreme magistrates (consuls), the aristocratic power of a permanent body of political initiative and deliberation (senate) and the popular exercise of power through representation (tribunes).[7]

In a perspective informed by its effective history and productive reception, Plato's *Republic* shows itself not to be the idealized portrayal of a particular city-state—of a particularly perfect city-state in the Greek tradition at that—but the outline of what the city-state as such, and by extension the state as such, or the state "in the idea" is all about: the public institution and administration of justice. From this formal and functional perspective on the republican idea, the doctrinal details of Plato's influential politico-philosophical dialogue are less interesting and not essential for ascertaining the systematic significance and the political presence of Plato's republic in the subsequent republican tradition.

The status of Plato's *Republic* as a clearly dated but continuously debatable model for how to think about the nature and function of a republican state also manifests itself in the generic identification of the republic with the state that can be found in later political thought. The term "republic" came to be employed for any state and city free from external political domination, such as the Northern Italian trade republics of late medieval and early modern times and the "free Imperial cities" of the German Empire, which were subordinate not to some local lord but only to the remote and largely ineffective political authority of the Emperor and moreover enjoyed regular representation among the estates of the empire. Occasionally, the term even covered cases of monarchical government, provided the latter was guided by rules or rule-like practices binding both the ruler and the ruled.[8]

Eventually the term "republic" was used for any well-ordered body politic not marked by arbitrary, despotic rule, effectively making the term coextensive with "state" in the latter's modern meaning as a territorially defined sovereign politico-juridical entity. The linkage to the republic of Roman descent and Platonic inspiration was the newly developing states' claimed concern with the common good making each of them, ideally, a "commonwealth," regardless of its often monarchical constitutional type. The term "republic" thus served to designate a mode of government by the rule of law and in the common interest rather than a particular constitution of political rule. At this point of its conceptual history, the generalized political designation "republic" could even be substituted by the modernized Greek name for both the state as such and for the state in its possible optimal form, "polity," derived from the Greek term *politeia.*

The identification of the Latin-based term "republic" with the Greek-based term "polity" had been preceded and prepared by Aristotle's use of the term *politeia* as an appellation for the altogether preferable political constitution.[9] Aristotle's linguistic choice may have been undertaken for the lack of a better, more closely descriptive term for the preferred political constitution that would allow distinguishing between the genus and a singled-out species. But the homonymy between the general term for the body politic and the specific name for its optimal form also links Aristotle back to Plato's dramatic foreshortening of the numerous forms of politic life to the ideal, perfect one as the only one that measures up to closer politico-philosophical scrutiny.

In addition to the widened usage of "republic" for the optimally constituted state, there had also been attempts in medieval and early modern times to restitute the particular profile of the Roman Republic under substantially changed conditions. Prominent examples of such revised revivals of republican thought and action were the medieval and early modern political opponents of any and all princely rule ("monarchomachs") that sought to curb and curtail royal and imperial power, as well the anti-monarchical and even regicidal factions in the era of the English Civil War, a political position based, in part, on a republican reading of the Hebrew Bible.[10] Further cases involving the claim to a modern return of republicanism in political theory and political practice are the civic virtue republicanism of humanism and Renaissance in Europe and Rousseau's Roman-republican transfiguration of Calvinist Geneva.[11]

But it was not until the bourgeois revolutions at the end of the eighteenth century, which turned America and France into republics in official name and strict form, that a republican constitution directly inspired by Roman history and indirectly shaped by the Platonic ideal of a republican state became a political reality under the form of a modern territorial state, rivaling and challenging the prevalence of monarchical rule in Europe and its colonial extensions. In the process, the old republics largely marked by patrician privilege were replaced, in theory as well as in practice, by democratic republics not based on direct, plebiscitarian popular rule as in ancient Athens but on the "representational system" that delegated deliberation and decision to a newly emerging class of committed citizens that eventually evolved into professional politicians.

But before republicanism turned indirectly-democratic, in the process replacing the political pursuit of the public good with the politics of maximizing the personal good of the individual citizen, the republican tradition along with its Platonic inspiration underwent a further transformation. This late set of variations on the republican theme of ethico-political self-rule, which was largely limited to theory and to speculative thought, can be found in the works of Kant and his idealist successors, chiefly among them Fichte and Hegel, each of whom looks back to the ancient precedent of Plato's *Republic* when attempting to forge a specifically modern political philosophy.[12]

Against the background of the emerging revolutionary political events in North America and Continental Europe and in critical engagement with modern political thought from Hobbes through Rousseau, classical German philosophy develops a distinct, if diverse, political philosophy that is at once attentive to recent developments in political ideas and in political reality and mindful of the normative basis of modern political reality in recognized rules (laws) governing individual, social and civic life. In particular, German political thinking from Kant through Fichte to Hegel chiefly concerns itself with the distinct but related normative regulations involved in personal ethics, in civil law and in public justice and focuses on the correlated tripartite legislation of "morality" (*Moralität*), of "private law" (*Privatrecht*) and of "public law" (*öffentliches Recht*), each deemed and designed to enable as much as condition the institution and exercise of political power in the state.

Placed against the twofold background of Plato's *Republic* and of the political tradition of republicanism, Kant, Fichte and Hegel, each in their own way, take up the Platonic-republican core concerns with the rule of law, with the public administration of justice and with the political exercise of self-governance. To be sure, the classical German contribution to modern political philosophy is significantly shaped by the German academic law tradition of preterpositive, "natural law" (*Naturrecht*) and by the peculiar German political situation: one of absolutist but regionally limited rule in a politically fragmented territorial conglomerate only nominally united by the anachronistic geographical term "Germany" and resembling more a federative republic of largely independent states than a centralized empire, much less an absolute monarchy.

Relating the political thought of Kant, Fichte and Hegel to its overt or covert engagement with Plato's *Republic* not only allows the identification of a distinctly modern tradition of republican political thinking in classical German philosophy—a largely juristic form of republicanism to be found in each of the three philosophers. The comparative contrast with Plato's *Republic* also brings out the specific differences between the contributions made to modern political thought by the three philosophers, as reflected in the mirror of their critical engagements and disengagements with Plato's *Republic*. While Kant's political philosophy looks back to Plato as a pre-Kantian idealist, Hegel construes him as reflecting an actual political *ethos* and Fichte draws on him for a radical vision of the political future.

Their considerable differences in philosophical positions and political philosophy notwithstanding, Kant, Fichte and Hegel agree in a specifically idealist philosophical outlook which ranks mind over matter, the spiritual over the material and the normative over the factual. It is this shared "German idealism," characteristically different from the historically antecedent British variety of idealism espoused by Berkeley in his refutation of independent material being, that makes Kant, Fichte and Hegel susceptible to and even appreciative of the transempirical, supranatural bent of Plato's philosophy in general and of Plato's political philosophy in particular. Not surprisingly then the sustained reflection on Plato's *Republic* in classical German political philosophy is framed by a more general appreciation of Platonic thinking in Kant, Fichte and Hegel.

There is one further feature that unites Kant, Fichte and Hegel in their political philosophy, while setting all three of them apart from Plato. German idealist political thought shares the characteristically modern concern with freedom in general and with the freedom of the individual human being in particular. But unlike the liberal legacy prevalent in British and British-inspired modern philosophy from Locke through J. S. Mill to the present, that links freedom primarily to individual choice,[13] classical German philosophy ties freedom foremost to self-legislation or autonomy and has the individual human being achieve self-realization in supraindividual contexts, chiefly among them civil society or the state.

The self-mastery and self-control involved in moral, social and civil acting under self-given but not selfishly given laws again links German idealist thinking, including its political thinking, to the

Platonic-republican legacy of acting under equitable laws rather than under arbitrarily chosen rules and regulations. The modern mark that the German idealists add to the ancient, essentially republican joining of freedom and lawfulness is the tie of freedom to self-legislation—the notion that human beings are free insofar as they act under laws that issue from their own considered legislative will, or that could so have arisen.

The inherent Platonism of classical German philosophy in general and the residual republicanism of classical German political philosophy in particular contrast markedly with the subsequent alternative orientation of modern moral philosophy and modern political philosophy toward Aristotle's *Ethics* and *Politics*, which have been especially influential in British and American philosophy from the late nineteenth century to the present. Conversely, in light of the Platonic and republican profile of Kantian and post-Kantian philosophy, the rising presence of Kantian and post-Kantian moral and political thought over the past decades indicates a Platonic countercurrent to the continuing Aristotelian revival and suggests a republican reorientation—even if nowadays the ideal has been transformed into the counterfactual, the unconditionally commanded into the normative and the republican *ethos* of self-mastery into the democratic culture of self-realization.

2

The Ideal Republic: Kant and Plato

"[A] government of Laws, not of Men"[1]

Ancients and Moderns

Comparing Plato and Kant and looking back from Kant to Plato at that—as the sequence of their names in the subtitle of this chapter suggests—might seem quite an unexpected, even unusual and perhaps unprofessional undertaking. To begin with, there are the established disciplinary divisions drawn between the different positions and periods of Western philosophy. To put it crudely: Kantians are not Platonists, and vice versa. The political focus of the proposed comparison, as indicated by the reference to a particular type or view of the state in the chapter's main title, "republic," could still appear more surprising. After all there are vast differences in outlook on things political that separate ancient Greek and modern European philosophical thought as well as classical Greek and modern European political reality. Yet the proposed philosophical comparison is motivated by Kant himself, who drew important inspiration from Plato, even as he set out to criticize him for his extravagant metaphysics and his elitist epistemology. In fact, Kant credited Plato with insights and discoveries to which he himself would lay claim, albeit under radically revised premises and fully aware of what separated his retake from his illustrious successor's original position.

The particular focus of the proposed comparison between Kant and Plato is on the political concept of "republic"—a term of art of Latin etymological origin (*res publica*) with remote roots in the Greek invention of the city-state (*polis*) and the design of its constitution (*politeia*). As detailed in the first chapter, the modern coinage of the term in the major European languages (English *republic*; French *république*; Italian *reppublica*; German *Republik*) and its modern use for the designation of a special kind of political rule is informed by the precedent of the Roman Republic, an originally aristocratic regime of Rome's patrician elite, with increasing popular representative participation.

The ubiquitous Roman political signature statement "SPQR," an abbreviation for the republican dualism of "the senate and the people of Rome" (*senatus populusque romanus*), conveys the proclaimed joint exercise of political rule by patricians and commoners. The republican constitution shaped Roman history in the five hundred years between the legendary expulsion of its kings and the historical establishment of its imperial rulers. When in later times the term and concept "republic" received a wider meaning and significance it served to designate and characterize a type of political rule purposively and pointedly removed from the whims of individuals (rulers such as kings and despots), kept free of the material and mental corruption associated with the arbitrary exercise of personal power and governed by generally binding rules or laws instead.[2]

The original conception of the republican constitution of a civil society or state—inspired by Rome, derived from Greece and revived in modern Europe and North America—provides a meeting ground for Kant's and Plato's political philosophy within the wider context of their philosophical oeuvre. While not a Platonist, Kant partakes in Plato's conception of the republican state as the ideal form and norm of political life. While not a Kantian, Plato shares Kant's assessment of the republican state as an optimal societal order to be emulated even if never achieved.

To be sure, Kant's congenial encounter with Plato across the divides of space and time cannot obscure the enormous differences between their philosophical conceptions of the state and between ancient Greek and modern European notions of political life in general. In fact, comparing Kant and Plato on the political ideal of the republic is apt to bring out clearly and distinctly not only what unites the two philosophers in their thinking about statehood and citizenship but also what sets them apart from each other in their different views about the purpose of political life and the relation between philosophy and the state.

The difference between Kant and Plato, specifically their divergence in matters of political philosophy, is a representative reflection of the difference between ancient and modern thinking about freedom and citizenship as well as between ancient and modern conceptions of a life worth living. Kant's espousal of Plato is genuine but limited. It concerns common lines of thought, chiefly involving the political role of laws—their supreme rule in political life. But it does not obliterate specific differences, which are centered around the divergent conceptions of freedom in ancient and modern thinking and living. Just as Plato, or any of the ancients—Greek or Roman—could not conceive of every human being's equal standing and unconditional worth, as the moderns characteristically would, so Kant, or any of the moderns—French, Dutch, British or German—could not fathom the irrevocable integration of the individual into a rigidly fixed station of political power (or powerlessness) and social rank (or lack thereof). On the whole, ancient and modern conceptions of freedom remain as different in Plato and Kant, as they present themselves in ancient and modern thought in general.

The Prehistory of the History of Philosophy

Although he made occasional references to historical philosophical figures, Kant was not a historian of philosophy.[3] In his pursuit of a characteristically critical thinking unencumbered by prejudice and tradition he even disparaged those to whom the history of philosophy was philosophy itself.[4] But neither were most of Kant's philosophical contemporaries knowledgeable of philosophy's own history, nor did they consider the history of philosophy an integral part of philosophy proper. It was Hegel who promoted the history of philosophy from an object of antiquarian curiosity to a core discipline of philosophy, based on the argument that philosophy, like the other manifestations of the world's governing principle ("spirit")—chiefly among them art, religion and philosophy, as well as right and law—involved the development of thought over time and across space in an extended historical process following its own structuring concepts ("logic"). Based on Hegel's logical historicism, the history of philosophy became an object of philosophical research in the nineteenth and twentieth centuries, originally among Hegel's own students and followers, a good number of whom made important contributions to the emerging philosophical field of the history of philosophy.

Still the beginnings of the Hegelian and post-Hegelian logico-historical treatment of philosophy's development can be detected already in Kant, specifically in his typological treatment of individual philosophers and entire philosophical schools. The systematic context for Kant's limited concern with historical philosophical positions is the self-interpretive project of locating his own philosophy, especially the critical revolution introduced into philosophy, in the context of antecedent authors and contemporary competitors.

At the core of Kant's philosophical concern with philosophy's history lies a general tripartite scheme that divides historical progress toward critical philosophy into a quasi-logical sequence running from dogmatism, chiefly exemplified by the Leibniz-Wolffian school philosophy of mid-eighteenth-century German academic teaching, through modern skepticism, as epitomized by David Hume's empiricism and naturalism, to criticism, advanced by Kant himself as a solution to the philosophical-historical stalemate between metaphysical extravagance and anti-metaphysical meekness.[5] So closed and complete is Kant's schema of the ultimately successful history of the three-staged development of philosophy that he envisions and even announces the imminent conclusion of a perpetual peace in philosophy, analogous to the world peace order he had sketched in his political philosophy under the influence of a contemporary peace agreement (Peace of Basel, 1795).[6]

While the chief representatives of philosophy's antecedent development stem from Kant's own century, ancient philosophy, including Plato, figures prominently in the sketchy historical account of the prior assessments of reason—of earlier, uncritical accounts of reason—that Kant offers on the very last pages of the *Critique of Pure Reason*, in the final section of the work's concluding part, titled "The History of Pure Reason."[7]

Referring to three "main revolutions"[8] in the history of philosophy, concerning the object, the origin and the method involved in cognition through reason (*Vernunft*), Kant cites Plato as the chief representative, first, of the intellectualist position that the true objects of rational cognition are not sensible entities to be encountered in space and time but intelligible beings to be grasped by the intellect alone, and, second, of the apriorist position that the origin of rational cognition does not lie in the senses but in reason itself, which is claimed to dispose of its own store of concepts possessed and employed independent of experience.

In both cases Kant connects Plato's position with the attribution, or rather the charge, of mysticism ("mystical," "mystical system").[9] The accusation concerns Plato's recourse to concepts of reason—the Forms (*ideai, eide*)—removed from ordinary knowledge and to be grasped only by some special and, on Kant's account, spurious intuition on the part of the intellect ("intellectual intuition"). The charge of mysticism against Plato can also be found elsewhere in Kant, chiefly in his unpublished literary remains (*Reflexionen*), when he reviews and assesses earlier attempts to account for the possibility of purely rational ("metaphysical") cognition and to assign a peculiar object domain to such putative knowledge based on reason alone.[10] The mysticism charge against Plato also figures in a late essay by Kant titled "Of a Recently Prominent Tone of Superiority in Philosophy" (1796),[11] in which Plato is adduced as the source of inspiration behind contemporary attempts to substitute the critical labor of distinguishing legitimate from illegitimate knowledge claims with the convenient appeal to an extraordinary source of insight into things that bypasses honest labor in favor of alleged preternatural inspiration.

But Kant's references to Plato are not limited to Plato's epistemology and metaphysics and not to severe criticisms of Plato's positions either. Outside of what he himself terms "theoretical philosophy"—philosophy concerned with the cognition of what there is—and specifically in "practical philosophy," involving the cognition of what there ought to be and comprising "moral philosophy" (*Moralphilosophie*) in the wider sense, consisting of ethics (*Ethik*) and right (juridical law; *Recht*),[12] Kant shows himself repeatedly appreciative of Plato's philosophical work, especially of

Plato's insistence on a kind of cognition not exhausted by empirical origins and objects. In fact, already in Kant's chief work in theoretical philosophy, the *Critique of Pure Reason*, which to a large part is an indirect, negative preparation, if not an outright grounding of his systematically subsequent moral philosophy, Kant seeks to redeem and rescue Plato from his own criticisms and charges by retrieving, or rather reconstructing, a Plato who in significant ways is akin to and ahead of Kant's own views on the metaphysical and epistemological foundations of ethics, law and politics.

From Categories to Ideas

Kant's retrieval of Plato occurs in one of the lesser-studied parts of the *Critique of Pure Reason*, the introductory chapter of the Transcendental Dialectic,[13] which precedes the detailed argumentative reconstructions and assessments of the core doctrines of rationalist philosophy on the three special topics of traditional metaphysics—soul, world and God. Before engaging in the threefold critique of rational psychology in the Paralogisms of Pure Reason, of rational cosmology in the Antinomy of Pure Reason and of rational theology in the Transcendental Ideal, Kant presents a general account of the logical instruments involved in traditional metaphysical thought and of the basic structure of reasoning underlying the particular claims of metaphysics to knowledge of entities that lie beyond the limits of space and time.

But the opening chapter of the Transcendental Dialectic, including its historical reference to Plato, prepares not only the subsequent negative critique of the metaphysical cognition of the soul, the world and God and the effective destruction of rationalist metaphysics altogether. Kant's account of the transcendental-logical concepts, principles and inferences underlying traditional metaphysics survives the latter's critical elimination and adds a significant further feature to the account and assessment of the nature and the reach of reason in the *Critique of Pure Reason*. More yet, Kant's general reflections on the transcendental logic of metaphysical reasoning at the beginning of the Transcendental Dialectic have lasting implications for the project that Kant pursues subsequent to the *Critique of Pure Reason* and on the basis of the latter's conceptual and doctrinal preparations—the grounding and building of a practical philosophy based on the demonstrated inadequacy of a purely naturalist account of the world and the human beings in it and involving the reassertion of a supranatural reality, chiefly the reality of radical freedom.

The key concept introduced into the critical account of reason at the beginning of the Transcendental Dialectic, with far-reaching consequences for Kant's entire further philosophical work, is that of the "idea" (*Idee*).[14] Kant presents ideas as concepts of reason, with "reason" (*Vernunft*) understood not in the generic sense of encompassing the entire intellect, or the "upper faculty of cognition," at the exclusion of the senses, but in the narrow sense of reason as the faculty of inferential thinking that proceeds from given parts to the corresponding wholes or, more generally, from the conditioned to the totality of its conditions or the unconditioned.

The exclusive linkage of ideas and reason (the latter taken in the narrow sense) makes Kant's concept of the idea the designated vehicle for metaphysical thinking—both for the fallacious recourse to ideas in traditional metaphysics and for their legitimate use envisioned already in the *Critique of Pure Reason* and executed in Kant's subsequent work in practical philosophy, chiefly under the guise of the idea of freedom. Moreover, the Kantian conception of ideas as concepts of reason forms a structural counterpart and a functional alternative to the pairing of the understanding with the categories—the latter understood as pure concepts of the understanding—in the Transcendental Analytic of the *Critique of Pure Reason*. While the categories, on Kant's construal, serve to understand the object domain of nature, in fact prescribing nature its laws based on the categorial forms, the ideas, according to Kant, in principle transcend and transgress the realm of nature and aim at entities essentially located beyond the natural world.[15]

Within the overall architectonic of the *Critique of Pure Reason*, Kant's introduction of concepts of reason or ideas—of ideas of pure reason, to be precise—in the Transcendental Dialectic is to be regarded as a counterpart, equal in innovation and importance, to the introduction of space and time as forms of intuition, and as pure intuitions in their own right, in the Transcendental Aesthetic. Earlier in the *Critique of Pure Reason* it proved crucial and consequential for the critical assessment of the reach of reason (the latter term understood in its wider sense as comprising the entire upper faculty of cognition, including understanding, the power of judgment and reason in the narrow sense) to distinguish space and time as forms of sensibility from the categories as concepts of the understanding and to eliminate space and time from the list of categories into which they had been included in general metaphysics or ontology since Aristotle.[16] Now it proves just as important for a proper grasp of the nature of reason to distinguish the categories as the concepts essentially suited to understanding nature from the ideas as the concepts essentially aiming beyond nature. In fact, the basic error of traditional, rationalist metaphysics, as diagnosed by Kant in the *Critique of Pure Reason*, can be described as the mistake of confusing the role and function of the concepts of reason (ideas) with those of the concepts of the understanding (categories) and of having ideas relate to their preternatural objects as though they were categories relating to natural objects.

From Plato's Ideas to Kant's Ideas

Kant's crucial recourse to Plato when introducing the concepts of reason or ideas in the opening of the Transcendental Dialectic is philosophically motivated and linguistically informed. Kant finds himself in need of a technical term suited for setting off the concepts of reason about to be investigated from other types of concepts, especially from the concepts of the understanding or the categories, previously investigated in the Transcendental Analytic of the *Critique of Pure Reason.* Rather than coining a new term, which would involve the "arrogation of legislation in linguistic matters," which he considers always fraught with risk, he resorts to an already existing term in a classical, "dead and learned" language that is suitably close in meaning and use to what the new term is intended to exhibit. Kant reports to have found such a term in Plato's originally Greek word for the "prototype" (*Muster*) of things, using its Germanized form, *Idee,* to render what in Plato is called, alternatively, *eidos* and *idea.*[17]

In English it has become customary to render Plato's Greek terms *idea* and *eidos* as "Form," typically capitalizing the word to indicate its status as a technical term. This serves to avoid confusing the Platonic idea with the modern meaning of the word "idea" as "representation," a usage that goes back to John Locke's *Essay Concerning Human Understanding*—in turn based on Descartes's word usage (Latin, *idea,* French, *idée*)—and its formative influence on modern Anglophone philosophy and philosophical terminology. By contrast, the standard German translation of the Greek terms *idea* and *eidos* has been *Idee,* whereas the modern sense of "idea" as "representation" is rendered by the word *Vorstellung.*[18]

In arguing for his recourse to Plato's "ideas"[19] to designate the concepts of reason, Kant points to the contrast between the status and role of the categories in accordance with Aristotle, which serve to bring out the conceptual determinations of objects of experience, located in space and time and cognitively accessible to the senses, and the status and role of the ideas according to Plato, which concern entities that lie beyond experience and that involve the mind in a world apart and entirely different from the ordinary realm of the senses. Rather than serving to spell out experience,[20] as the categories can be seen to do in Aristotle (and in Kant's own account of them in the Transcendental Analytic), ideas serve to intentionally and purposively transcend all experience and are therefore indicative of a dimension of reality that lies beyond the reach of the senses. General speaking, ideas reflect a fundamental dissatisfaction on the part of reason with the limits of the categorial understanding and its world of empirical objects.

Still Kant does not adopt Plato's characterization of ideas entirely. In particular, he critiques Plato's "mystical" bent in treating ideas as objects of their own and as involving a kind of object that is superior to ordinary empirical objects at that. In characterizing Plato's ideas as "archetypes of the things themselves" (*Urbilder der Dinge selbst*)[21] Kant even suggests an identity of sorts between Platonic ideas and the "things in themselves," the latter of which the *Critique of Pure Reason* relegates to the sphere of what is and always will remain unassailable to human, essentially limited cognitive efforts.

Kant further cites disapprovingly the Platonic characterization of the ideas as "emanating from the highest reason,"[22] which would effectively locate them in a divine intellect. While this attribution might be more pertinent to neo-Platonic emanatist metaphysics than to Plato himself, its origin can be traced to Plato's *Timaeus.* Kant, though, mentions neither source, but moves on to Plato's account of human knowledge as a dim "recollection"[23] of the originary, divine vision of things—a position traceable to Plato's doctrine of recollection (*anamnesis*) as presented in the *Meno,* although, again,

Kant cites or mentions no specific source.

In line with his strictly instrumental interest in the history of philosophy, Kant is not intent on engaging in detailed analyses or protracted speculations about Plato's intent and purpose in maintaining and defending extravagant claims on the nature and knowledge of ideas. Rather than getting involved in the historical exegesis, the argumentative analysis and the philosophical assessment of Plato's texts ("literary investigation"),[24] Kant moves directly to developing a philosophical reading and reconstruction of what Plato says about ideas that shows the latter to be in considerable conformity with the main tenets of the critical philosophy.

Kant justifies his abrupt move away from the doctrinal views on the ideas attributable to Plato, with which he has taken issue from a critical point of view, to the strategically motivated retrieval of Plato as a main source of inspiration for his own account of the ideas by adducing a hermeneutic *topos.* As Kant reminds his readers, it is not unusual for someone else to understand an author better than he was able to understand himself. According to Kant, the exegetical surplus value to be gained by one or more readers of, or listeners to, an author's presented views is due to those readers' or listeners' extraneous position, which allows them to collate and compare the author's views in their multiple and varied presentations, to identify and address any remaining ambiguity and indetermination in them and to extract a defensible core meaning that may well have eluded the original author but which could be considered to be actually contained and effectively manifest in what the author himself said or wrote.[25]

Equipped with this hermeneutic maxim, Kant proceeds to a selective revisionist, essentially critical appropriation of Plato for which he claims a basis in Plato's own pronouncements, arguing that their elevated diction, involving the hypostatization of ideas into suprasensible superobjects, is capable of a "milder interpretation more appropriate to the nature of things."[26] The point of departure for Kant's rereading of Plato is the observation that Plato resorts to ideas mainly in practical matters involving a kind of cognition allied with human conduct and including a "proper product of reason."[27] By contrast, Kant dismisses explicitly Plato's use of ideas in theoretical matters, specifically their employment in mathematics, citing as his reason for so doing the fact, established in the earlier parts of the *Critique of Pure Reason,* that the sole concern of mathematics is with the intuitional forms of objects in space and tine ("mathematics of appearances")[28] and not with the properties of things beyond the domain of space and time.

The initial limitation to ideas concerning practical matters allows Kant to focus on a single defining feature of ideas in Plato: their counterfactual status, which makes the ideas involved in practical matters—essentially in human conduct and the cognitions that guide it—unsuitable for validation by appeal to past and present experiences. For the latter can only provide instances and examples and are unable to determine or affect the status of ideas as the (claimed) archetypes of any and all human conduct. The chief idea in Plato concerning practical matters cited approvingly by Kant is that of "virtue" (*Idee der Tugend*), taken as the core concept for human conduct under the guidance of an archetype that at once informs and motivates human action. Kant stresses that, while the "idea of virtue" may never be adequately instantiated in actual human conduct, it is not therefore empty and illusory ("chimerical"), but quite to the contrary the very necessary condition of "all judgment about moral worth or unworth" and of "all approximation to moral perfection."[29]

In addition to endorsing ideas involving the orientation and motivation of human conduct, Kant also cites approvingly Plato's employment of ideas in natural philosophy. More specifically, he contrast the merely "imitative contemplation" (*copeiliche Betrachtung*)[30] of nature through the categorial understanding, which remains limited to grasping what is physical about the order of things, with the teleological and architectonic consideration of nature involving the purposive structure and functioning of its individual products as well as its overall design—an organization of nature that can be considered to have its "origin in ideas."[31] According to Kant, those original ideas are located by Plato in a divine intellect and are always only inadequately realized by any given object and order of nature. While chastising Plato for his extravagant claims on insight into the particulars of the divine master plan of nature, Kant approves of the "spiritual up-soar of the philosopher" (*Geistesschwung des Philosophen*)[32] from the sensible to the supersensible and from the physical to the metaphysical that finds expression in the teleological consideration of nature. On Kant's assessment, such a supranatural consideration of nature is reflective of the "proper dignity of philosophy," and Plato deserves "respect and emulation"[33] for its introduction into philosophy.

The common feature uniting Kant's mitigated endorsement of practical ideas (concerning human conduct) and of architectonic ideas (concerning the purposiveness of nature) in Plato is the notion of a causality on the part of ideas by means of which ideas are, or are to be regarded as, bringing about something—human actions in the case of practical ideas and natural objects in that of architectonic ideas. To be sure, the former type of idea-causality involves a finite, human intellect, while the latter one presupposes an infinite intellect. A further disanalogy explicitly stated by Kant concerns the distinctive role of practical ideas, which "first make the experience (of the good) itself possible"[34] in that they are capable of bringing about actions and objects more or less congruent with the standard of perfection encapsulated in a practical idea.

After the opening consideration of the Transcendental Dialectic on ideas in general, with significant references to Plato, Kant moves on to a specific account of the three sets of ideas that underlie metaphysical reasoning and that are prone to lead to fallacious conclusions and erroneous doctrines on the nature of the soul, the constitution of the world and the existence and essence of God. By contrast to the practical and architectonic ideas introduced before, the three "transcendental ideas" regarding the soul, the world and God are theoretical in nature and concern the cognition of objects—more precisely, the alleged knowledge of supersensory entities.

Like the other types of ideas (practical and architectonic) taken over from Plato, the transcendental ideas are to be considered "products of reason"—although not in the Platonic sense of originating in divine reason but in the Kantian sense of having their origin in human reason as such, independent of experience (a priori). Yet the purely rational origin of transcendental ideas in Kant is not a matter of factual first beginnings, as though ideas were products of mental acts. Rather they are to be regarded as the logical forms and conditions for any such mental acts. Ideas in Kant are not mental items, akin to Lockean ideas. They may not be objects *sui generis,* in the manner of Plato's ideas. But they still are objective and logical in their status and to that extent remain closer to Plato's ontology of ideas-as-Forms than to Locke's psychology of ideas-as-representations.

From Plato's Republic to Kant's Republic

Kant's critical assessment of Plato's ideas, characteristically divided between rejection and adoption, in the opening chapter of the Transcendental Dialectic of the *Critique of Pure Reason* culminates in an appreciative account of the "Platonic republic" (*Platonische*

Republik).[35] Kant takes issue with the proverbial characterization of Plato's work on the ideal state as an egregious example of "dreamed-up perfection that can reside only in the brain of the idle thinker" and with the widespread mockery of the notion to be found in Plato's work that "a prince will never rule well unless he participates in the ideas."[36] Rather than to dismiss Plato's political thoughts on these alleged grounds, Kant recommends sustained reflection on them and to supplement their justification, which might be missing or lacking in Plato himself, with "new endeavors."[37]

Kant's own reconstruction of the core meaning and message of "the Platonic republic," which immediately follows upon his apologetic argument, reads Plato's republic as a "necessary idea" that is to be considered not only in the first founding of a "state constitution" (*Staatsverfassung*) but also in all the state's subsequent "legislation" (*Gesetzgebung*).[38] Kant concedes that "initially" (*anfänglich*) one might have to abstract from all kinds of obstacles that seem to impede if not inhibit the political effectiveness of the republican idea. But he also suggests that the obstacles in question might not stem from "human nature," which would make them inevitable, but could be indicative of the disregard, prevalent so far, for the very idea of a state's republican constitution and hence susceptible of correction and improvement.

Kant takes issue with the "appeal to allegedly contrary experience"[39] in the widespread dismissal of ideas such as that of the Platonic republic. According to Kant, this narrowly empiricist attitude even causally contributes to the practical ideas' ineffectiveness in practice and so consolidates the prevalence of experience contrary to those ideas. Kant concedes that any and all approximation to the Platonic idea of the republic will remain finite and incomplete. But he is equally convinced that the exact extent of the eventually remaining discrepancy between the idea and its execution cannot be determined in advance and that the "highest degree of perfection at which humanity must stop"[40] is an open issue to be determined not by past experience but by the future course of history.

Kant's functional reading of Plato's republic-in-the-idea focuses throughout on the latter's counterfactual status—its orientational role and motivational capacity for future politics. While this interpretation of Plato's *Republic* is entirely in line with Kant's general understanding of Plato's ideas, it neither exhausts nor even addresses Plato's further specifications of the ideal republic, nor does it exhaust what Kant believes himself able to extract from Plato in matters of political philosophy.

Anyone only slightly familiar with Plato's *Republic* (the work itself not its project, which is referred to by Kant with the descriptive phrase "the Platonic republic") must be surprised, even taken aback by the way in which Kant defines the idea of the republic in the context of the introduction of ideas in the Transcendental Dialectic, calling it "a constitution of the greatest human freedom according to laws which provide that the freedom of each can coexist with that of the others" (*eine Verfassung von der größten menschlichen Freiheit nach Gesetzen, welche machen, daß jedes Freiheit mit der andern ihrer zusammen bestehen kann*).[41] This certainly is not Plato's understanding of the ideal city-state (*polis*) and its constitution (*politeia*) in the work titled, in the customary English translation, *The Republic.*

Neither the concept of human freedom, specifically that of freedom in the political sphere, nor the latter's possession and exercise by all, nor its restriction by laws designed to ensure everyone's freedom are to be found in Plato. In fact these are notions entirely alien to Plato—and to the ancient world in general. To be sure, Plato's ideal republic aims at the establishment and the maintenance of justice (*dikaiosyne*) in the political sphere, along with the introduction and preservation of other politically salient positive character traits or virtues (*aretai*) such as wisdom (*sophia*), courage (*andreia*) and moderation (*sophrosyne*). But the political virtues are to be distributed among the different classes or estates in the ideal city-state (rulers, guardians, the wider populace) or are to pertain to the political whole, respectively. Plato's republic is not a free state consisting of human beings who may freely choose what they do. The laws governing Plato's republic are not designed for, and restricted to, the establishment of the conditions for maximizing everyone's freedom and for minimizing everyone's and the state's interference in everyone else's actions.

But a closer look at the text reveals that Kant is not actually claiming to follow Plato with his quintessentially modern, not to say liberal specification of the idea of a republic. Rather Kant draws on Plato's *formal* analysis of the status and function of ideas in general and of the idea of "the Platonic republic" in particular for attributing those formal features to Kant's own modern conception of the state as a state of freedom under laws. The point of Kant's reference to "the Platonic republic" is not to claim Plato's political conception as his own, or to impose his own conception on Plato. Rather Kant aims to introduce the notion inspired by "the Platonic republic" that a genuinely philosophical treatment of the state, and of political matters in general, is not to be based on empirical concepts and historical experiences but on concepts generated by reason that are to be brought to bear on reality in the manner of practical laws and political precepts—in short, by ideas. Considered that way, Kant's recourse to Plato is not a historical reference to an earlier author and text, to be assessed for its accuracy and adequacy, but part of a methodological argument for the place of ideas in philosophy in general and in practical philosophy, including political philosophy, in particular.

Kant's Republicanism

The juridico-political conception of the state's original constitution and subsequent conservation as an enabler of everyone's freedom to be found in the *Critique of Pure Reason* under the guise of "the Platonic republic" is the core idea behind the political philosophy and the philosophy of law that Kant was to develop and publish in the ensuing two decades: from the essay on the philosophy of political history "Idea for a Universal History with a Cosmopolitan Intent" (1784)[42] through the critique of political eudemonism in section 2 of *On the Common Saying* (1793),[43] the fictitious peace accord *Toward Perpetual Peace* (1795)[44] and the defense of political progress in part 2 of *Conflict of the Faculties* (1798)[45] to the late critical philosophy of law and right in the "Metaphysical First Principles of the Doctrine of Right" of *The Metaphysics of Morals* (1797).[46]

In those later works Kant specifies further the kind and extent of freedom involved in the juridico-political sphere: it is external freedom in the exercise of human arbitrary choice (*Willkür*), as opposed to the inner freedom characteristic of ethical obligation. He further specifies the systematic linkage between law and power: someone's positive right to freely do something involves the state's negative right of constraint with regard to any hindrances of the legitimate exercise of that person's freedom by anyone else. He also specifies the nature of the obligation to enter into civil society or the state: it is an unconditional obligation neither motivated nor justified by fear or hope but categorically commanded as the necessary condition for guaranteeing right and realizing freedom. Finally, he specifies the constitution of the state that best ensures the rule of law and the exercise of freedom: it is an order marked by the distinction between the legislative and the executive power.

There is no reason to assume that Kant could foresee already in the *Critique of Pure Reason* the further detailed development that his philosophical thinking about law and politics was to take in the 1780s and 1790s, first in the context of his emerging mature moral philosophy, as manifested in the *Foundations of the Metaphysics of Morals* (1785) and the *Critique of Practical Reason* (1788), then in the context of his complex critical reaction to the French Revolution and the Revolutionary Wars involving large parts of Europe. On the contrary, textual evidence to be gathered from Kant's unpublished notes (*Reflexionen*) and from student transcripts of his lectures (*Vorlesungsnachschriften*) from the early 1780s suggests that the development of Kant's political philosophy and philosophy of law was a protracted process of productive engagement with the academic traditions of natural law, with the writings of Jean-Jacques Rousseau on science, culture and politics and with the revolutionary political events of 1789 and after.[47]

Still two key features of Kant's presentation of the idea of a state's constitution under the guide of "the Platonic republic" in the *Critique of Pure Reason* remain in place and even assume central importance in Kant's elaborated later philosophy: the indispensability of practical ideas in political philosophy and the philosophy of law, which lends a counterfactual, normative and prescriptive character to Kant's account of civil society or the state; and the final end of political society or the state being the enabling of freedom through laws that are as much expressive of freedom as they are protective of it.

Moreover, Kant's subsequent views and works on juridico-political matters continue to resort in important ways to the very term, "republic," which Kant initially had employed in reference to the Latinized title of Plato's work on the ideal state. The later Kant lends a twofold, related meaning to the term. Taken in the generic sense, "republic" in Kant is coextensive with "state" (*Staat*),[48] with the proviso that the term "state" addresses primarily the political authority of civil society—mainly in relation to other states—while the term "republic" is used chiefly for addressing the inner composition of civil society as a society of citizen-subjects. In this general sense, the concept "republic" does not refer to a particular kind of constitution obtaining in a given state. In Kant's technical vocabulary, this is the "republic in the wider sense" (*res publica latius dicta*).[49]

The specific meaning of "republic" to be found in Kant's later writings, notably from the 1790s and hence postdating the outbreak and unfolding of the French Revolution, refers to a particular constitution of the state, for which the term indicates defining features and functional requirements. In particular, Kant names the following "republican" features: the constitutional separation between the legislative and executive powers in a state, the freedom of the subjects from arbitrary laws, the equality of the citizens before the law and the independence of the citizens from conditions of tutelage and paternalism.[50]

The list of features characterizing a state that can be called "republican" in its organization as well as operation places Kant's political philosophy in the ancient and early modern tradition of republicanism, chiefly characterized by the rejection of despotism, corruption and civil inequality. The historical basis of political republicanism is to be found in aristocratic or patrician regimes, from the Roman Republic through the medieval and early Northern Italian city-states to the Federated Dutch Provinces and their successor, the Batavian Republic. The theoretical reflection on the republican tradition is provided by the classical Roman historians, chiefly Livy, by Machiavelli's retake on Livy, the *Discorsi,* and by Montesquieu's portrayal of republican rule in a world-historical comparative perspective.[51]

But Kant's conception of a republican constitution also differs significantly from antecedent accounts and assessments. In particular, Kant's endorsement of republicanism is theoretical and, so to speak, Platonic. He neither advocates nor encourages the overthrow of the existing political order in favor of establishing an actual republic. Rather he seeks to extract from the republican tradition in philosophy and politics a "spirit"[52] (*Geist, anima*) of republicanism that is to animate any given political order in the hope and with the expectation that the inward, spiritual or virtual republicanism initiates and contributes to a process of incremental republicanization of the state in its outer shape and form as well. In particular, Kant distinguishes between the constitutional setup or "state form" (*Staatsform*), which specifies the state's structure with regard to the political powers, and the "mode of governance" (*Regierungsart*) of a state or the manner, mind-set or "spirit" in which the state is governed.[53] With regard to the possible forms of the state Kant follows the politico-philosophical tradition, distinguishing the monarchical (Kant prefers the term "autocratic"),[54] the aristocratic and the democratic outer form of the state. He does not follow the tradition from Polybius onward, though, which advocates a "mixed constitution."

Given Kant's rejection of aristocratic privilege in favor of merit as a criterion for political office and power and his (and his contemporaries') profound distrust of popular rule, equated with majoritarian despotism,[55] Kant effectively favors the monarchical form of the state, provided the latter is governed by laws issued and applied with equity and in consideration of every citizen's equal freedom. The rule of law in turn depends on the mode in which the (outwardly monarchical) state is governed—whether in a "despotic" manner inimical to conditions of freedom and equality, instead involving arbitrary legislative, executive and jurisdictional power, or in a "republican" manner guided by the principle of everyone's equal freedom and the state's juridico-political obligation to treat everyone according to the "spirit of the laws of freedom" (*Geist der Freiheitsgesetze*).[56]

While Kant does not advocate or endorse republican revolutions, he welcomes their beneficial outcome, including their long-term effect on reformist political change in neighboring monarchical states. To be sure, the political changes for the better to be hoped for, to be expected and to be advanced are to take place "from above," as measures on the part of monarchical rulers and the increasingly enlightened executive branch of the monarchical state (magistrates).[57] According to Kant, an important factor in this process of monarchical self-republicanization is the critical public or the community of learned and committed citizens, who seek to advance enlightenment about theoretical and practical matters—chiefly among them science, religion and politics—through publication and conversation. Kant stresses the need for such a forum and its right to voice criticism even in political matters, provided the civil peace is not disturbed or threatened by it.[58]

Compared to the extensive, even excessive amount of political freedom demanded or enacted by republican thinkers and politicians of the past and in Kant's own time, some of whom even advocated or practiced revolution and regicide, Kant's intra-monarchical reformist republicanism may seem limited and timid. For the citizens of Kant's monarchically reigned and republicanly governed state are lawgivers "in the idea" only and have their ideal legislative power exercised in a "representational system."[59] Moreover, their political representation is not the result of popular electoral processes but based on the official appointment of persons or a body of persons charged with representing the political will of the citizens, in effect acting on their behalf by passing as well as enacting only laws to which the citizens could have given their (fictional) consent.

In redefining republicanism through political representation rather than through political participation, Kant has effectuated a significant departure from the ancient and early-modern republican tradition, for which the active inclusion of all qualified citizens into the political process was a definitional feature of the free state and its governance through the self-rule of the citizenry. As a consequence of Kant's representative and virtual turn in republicanism, the citizens in Kant lack the thorough involvement in politics characteristic of traditional, Roman and neo-Roman republicanism. The Kantian citizen is a subject freely obedient to laws of his own fictional making, committed to following the law, even knowledgeable of its justificatory basis, but not actively involved in its issue and imposition.

The Kantian citizen, while politically powerful only indirectly and fictitiously, through "representation," disposes though of a large measure of freedom of another kind than the one proudly claimed and exercised by the republican citizens of old, whose life was—or was seen as being—almost entirely dedicated to the conduct of politics. The classical Greeks even coined a verb for the sustained activity of energetic service to the *polis*, *politeuein* ("being engaged in things political"), and spoke disparagingly of a life led in private (*idioteuein*), because they considered the politically idle citizen useless and even burdensome.[60] By contrast, the citizen in Kant's ideal, virtual republic is a citizen of a primarily legal order—a juridical rather than a political republic—that enables and ensures the maximal exercise of everyone's personal rights. In Kant's philosophy of law, "public law" (*öffentliches Recht*), by regulating the structure and function of the state, serves to render communally compatible the individual personal entitlements afforded by "private law" (*Privatrecht*). The latter in turn is based on "natural law" (*Naturrecht*) or the "law of reason" (*Vernunftrecht*), which thus provides the justificatory basis and the ultimate end for the state's primarily juridical function—the effective protection of everyone's prepolitical, "natural" equal right to freedom by the means of politics.[61]

The personal freedom enabled by Kant's state of law is a typically modern freedom, no longer determined by traditional standards of social conduct and communal regimentation. It is the freedom of the individual, cherished in the modern world to the point of serving as one of its defining features, but much less appreciated, to a considerable extent quite unknown, in earlier times and in those parts of today's world less informed or persuaded by the conditions of modernity. Yet while the modern freedom of the individual is not the traditional republican freedom *for* the political life, it is a freedom that is largely owed to a specific, essentially republican conception of politics—a politics conducted in consideration of the political interests of equally free citizens.

It bears mentioning that the freedom to which Kant's modern, republican-minded state entitles and enables its citizens is not simply the negative freedom of a faculty of choice (*Willkür*) unencumbered by external strictures and restrictions. On Kant's account, the space of personal freedom granted to modern citizens—the citizens of a modern republic—is a space provided for an extended and multilayered educational process that is to occur by each individual's own cognitive and volitional efforts. In particular, the called-for theoretico-practical self-perfection of the human being comprises the perfectioning of technical skills, of civico-political manners and of ethico-moral attitudes. Kant distinguishes these three levels of individual self-development as the cultivation, the civilization and the moralization of the human being, arguing that the first two processes are well under way in his own time, while the latter has barely begun.[62]

There is a danger lurking behind the largely liberating differentiation of the political and the personal, the private and the public in modern life that manifests itself in Kant's republic. The increased dissociation of the personal from the political and of the private from the public risks to sever modern life from its political prerequisite in a republican-minded polity that prides itself on the freedom of its citizens. The newly freed modern citizen risks to get implicated, if not immersed, in apolitical self-regarding individualism and its indistinguishable counterpart, conformist collectivism. In the process, the ideal or virtual republic envisioned by Kant under the inspiration of Plato threatens to turn into the despotism of commerce and consumption. Faced with this postrepublican scenario, reading Plato through Kant can be part of the cultural formation and civic education needed to remind citizens that they are more than wage earners and income spenders and that life is larger than the pursuit of personal possessions and private preferences might make it seem.

3

The Real Republic: Hegel and Plato

"La politique, voilà le destin."[1]

Philosophy and Its History

Proposing to compare Hegel and Plato on the state—or the "republic," to use the title derived from the Latin language and from Roman politics for the civil community (*res publica*)—has some initial plausibility. For Plato and Hegel share a basic idealist outlook on natural and social reality, ranking thinking over sensing and intellectual entities over sensory objects. In fact, they could be considered the most prominent proponents and the most radical representatives of philosophical idealism in the ancient and in the modern world, respectively. Moreover, Plato and Hegel resemble each other quite closely in the dominant focus of their work in practical philosophy on the state and its central role in the shaping of human social life. Not surprisingly then, both Plato and Hegel have been regarded—or rather disregarded—as proponents of a strong, even overbearing state inimical to freedom and equality.[2]

But upon closer inspection and reflection, the apparent proximity between Plato and Hegel in general and between Plato and Hegel on the state in particular dissolves into difference and divergence. To be sure, there is a certain continuity between them due to their shared methodological conviction of the profoundly procedural nature of logical thinking ("dialectic"). Yet Plato presents his philosophy in dialogues that replace direct and authoritative doctrinal pronouncements with the indirect, polyphonic enactment of dissenting views and contradictory arguments. By contrast, Hegel lends his philosophy the inner and outer form of a logical system endowed with an elaborate architecture and supplied with detailed doctrines. Plato resorts to myths. Hegel relies on concepts. Plato has the interlocutors of his dialogues, chiefly among them Socrates, stress the yearning of philosophy for a world beyond the here and now. Hegel assigns to philosophy the task of reconciling human beings with the place and time of their situated existence. In Plato, the state ("republic") is presented as an ideal—a remote and unreachable archetype. In Hegel, the state figures as already accomplished and fulfilled, only waiting to be completely understood and philosophically appreciated. Most importantly, Plato's republic partakes in the political order of the ancient world, marked by naturally based social and civic distinctions. Hegel's philosophical portrayal of the state is directed specifically at the modern state.

In spite of these differences—or rather, precisely because of them—the contrastive comparison between Plato's and Hegel's philosophy of the state can be instructive and illuminating, especially if it is not carried out from a detached, third and neutral perspective but from within, as a regard on Plato through the eyes of Hegel and as a perspective on Plato's republic informed by Hegel's state. Such a directed comparison under the guise of Hegel's regard for Plato is apt to bring out more clearly what unites and what distinguishes Plato and Hegel, at least from Hegel's perspective, and to contribute to a better understanding if not of Plato than at least of Plato according to Hegel.

Hegel's critical treatment of Plato's philosophy in general and of Plato's political philosophy in particular is extensive and detailed. Unlike earlier philosophers, including his own mediate predecessor Kant, Hegel showed a profound interest in the history of philosophy, chiefly in European philosophy from the pre-Socratics to his own time, but also including Asian philosophy, specifically Indian, Chinese and Persian philosophical thought. But unlike the contemporaneous editors, translators and interpreters of historical philosophical authors, chiefly those from Greek and Roman antiquity, Hegel is not interested in the history of philosophy for antiquarian reasons and from a philological point of view. Rather Hegel's intensive interest in the history of philosophy is philosophical in character and deeply shaped by his own philosophical views.[3]

For Hegel the history of philosophy is not a historical matter, to be relegated to the margins of philosophy as a collection of curiosities about ancient authors and their antiquated views, but an integral part of philosophy's development as a system of knowledge with the status of a science (*Wissenschaft*). According to Hegel, the history of philosophy is philosophy itself as it develops from earlier, less adequate to later, increasingly adequate realizations of its core conception—the presentation of the absolute or unconditioned as the original unity of thinking and being, of the real and the ideal, of subject and object, of the natural world and the human world. Moreover, the absolute unity, for Hegel, is not to be regarded as static and fixed but as dynamic and developmental, with thinking turning into being, the ideal becoming real, the subject objectifying itself and the natural world going over into the human world.

The theoretical reflection of this logical as well as ontological world process is the internal development of philosophy as a successively unfolding series of insight into the historically manifest nature of the absolute. For Hegel, the historical development of the absolute is logical in nature, being not a matter of contingency and chance but the result of a transformative process primarily structured by logical concepts ("categories") and only secondarily taking place in space and over time. Accordingly, for Hegel, philosophical authors of the past are not past philosophical authors but developmental stages, specifically conditioned aspects or distinct logical moments in philosophy's teleological development to an ever more adequate, logically articulated presentational realization of the absolute.

Just as Hegel sought to detect reason in world history, tracing its logical development from the ancient, pagan world to the modern, essentially Christian world of his own time, so he set out to exhibit reason in the history of philosophy by identifying in authors of the distant and recent past the cumulative contributions to making philosophy ever more adequate to its task as finally understood and comprehensively undertaken by Hegel himself. What interests Hegel in the philosophers of the past and shapes his interpretive readings and philosophical interpretations of their views are the specific standpoints from which they address philosophy's general task. Hegel's concern is with their particular contributions to the overall development of philosophy, not with their shortcomings in contributing always only partially and inadequately to the remote end of philosophy, as conclusively revealed in its true form and utter completion in Hegel's system of philosophy.

Hence Hegel's philosophical relation to the history of philosophy is assimilationist and integrationist; he seeks out and appreciates, even praises in philosophers of the past what contributes to philosophy's logical advance from Heraclitus to Hegel. But he is also critical and even dismissive of earlier philosophers, when noting and highlighting the limited views and restricted horizons that prevented them from the complete and comprehensive vision to be achieved on the basis of the earlier efforts when considered in their entirety and sequence.

An instructive example and also a special case of Hegel's limited but sincere appreciation of the philosophers of the past is his critical presentation of Plato's philosophy in general and of Plato's political philosophy, as contained in "the books on the 'republic,'"[4] in particular. Hegel's reading of Plato is indicative and illustrative of his skillfulness and resourcefulness in identifying elements and anticipations ("moments") of the future final shape of philosophy. Most importantly, Hegel's reading of Plato includes the latter's defense against historical and contemporary attacks on his idealist philosophy in general and his idealist political philosophy in particular. But Hegel's account of Plato also is unusual for the extent of identification with Plato in which he engages. In fact, Hegel presents Plato as the very first form of philosophy that is true to the latter's systematic, scientific and speculative nature to be revealed in its final form only by Hegel himself.

Among the accusations addressed at Plato that Hegel reports and retorts is the charge of the comparative lack of originality of his philosophy, its eclectic and syncretistic character, based on the fact that Plato draws extensively, albeit quite creatively, on prior philosophers, from Parmenides through the Pythagoreans to his teacher Socrates.[5] Hegel concedes the doctrinal dependence, turning it into an advantage and a mark of attractiveness by arguing that Plato's philosophy represents the "knot" (*Knoten*)[6] in which the previously diverse and divergent philosophical developments are tied together and brought into a complex and compatibilist unity. This picture, applied by Hegel to Plato, also describes Hegel's own relation to the history of philosophy, which he at once inherits and improves, continues and concludes.

So far goes Hegel's historical identification with Plato that he organizes his main critical account of Plato's philosophy, in the Berlin lectures on history of philosophy first published posthumously in

1833, along the same lines as his own philosophical system, previously presented in the Heidelberg and Berlin versions of the *Encyclopedia of the Philosophical Sciences.*[7] In exact correspondence to the latter's tripartite division into logic, philosophy of nature and philosophy of mind or spirit (*Geist*), Hegel's presentation of Plato in the Lectures on the History of Philosophy is divided into three sections, following a lengthy introductory part surveying the status and significance of Plato's philosophy.[8]

The first part of the chapter on Plato titled "Dialectic" outlines the logical and ontological basic traits of Plato's philosophy, focusing on the late dialogues *The Sophist, Philebus* and *Parmenides* and employing the term "dialectic" introduced by Plato and appropriated by Hegel for the methodological self-description of thoughts-in-movement.[9] The second part is titled "philosophy of nature" (*Naturphilosophie*) and deals exclusively with Plato's late work in cosmology, the *Timaeus.*[10] The third and final part of the section on Plato bears the title "Philosophy of Spirit" (*Philosophie des Geistes*) and focuses almost entirely on Plato's practical philosophy, as presented in *The Republic,* with one reference to Plato's other main work in political philosophy, *The Laws.*[11]

The Real and the Ideal

The parallels to be drawn between Plato and Hegel—indications of a proximity between differently situated philosophers whose views, while never intersecting, remain forever close to each other—reach beyond the identical architectonic disposition of their chief philosophical concerns with logic, nature and mind (or spirit), as detailed by Hegel. The two philosophers share a focus on the "idea"—the term introduced by Plato into philosophy (*idea, eidos*) and taken up, some twenty-two centuries later, by Hegel as the key concept for his systematic philosophy and its philosophical system (*Idee*). In the meantime, Plato's primary term had been transposed into Latin (*idea*; same spelling, different accent) and eventually used to designate the mental matter that refers to extramental entities, as opposed to those entities themselves. Ideas, once in Plato the prototypical beings residing outside of space and time in an "overheavenly place" (*topos hyperouranios*), had become intramental items representing possible extramental entities, the synonym of "idea" now being "representation" (Latin, *repraesentatio*).

So profound is the gap that separates the later, essentially modern appropriation and adaptation of Plato's linguistic invention and philosophical discovery that it became indicated to use a different term for ideas in the older, now obsolete sense introduced by Plato, in order to avoid confusing ideas in Plato with those to be found in Descartes and his followers as well as critics, who did philosophy by "way of the ideas." The alternative English term for ideas in Plato became "Form," based on the literal, pre-philosophical meaning of the other of Plato's two terms for his ideas, "*eidos*," which is "aspect" or "view."

But it was not only the term "idea" that underwent comprehensive changes, including a radical reversal of meaning from designating entities altogether different from mind as well as matter to representational mental items. The term "idealism" derived from "idea" and originally designating Plato's metaphysical position, according to which ultimately only ideas have being, while everything else has being only in a tenuous sense, also underwent redefinition. It now served to designate the view, sometimes put forth tentatively, for argumentative purposes, sometimes actually affirmed and argued for, that the only things that can be shown and known to exist are ideas, the latter term understood in the non-Platonic, modern sense designating mental representations. George Berkeley famously declared there to be no being other than represented being (*esse est percipi*), specifically denying the independent reality of matter (immaterialism).

So prominent was the idealism assumed for skeptical reasons, as in Descartes, or asserted for dogmatic reasons, as in Berkeley, that Kant included the "refutation" of either idealism into the *Critique of Pure Reason.* Hew undertook to refute Berkeleyan, "dogmatic" idealism through his account of the empirical reality of space and time in the Transcendental Aesthetic[12] and Cartesian, "skeptical" idealism first in the Fourth Paralogism of Pure Reason of the first edition,[13] and then in the explicitly so-called Refutation of Idealism inserted into the Transcendental Analytic of the second edition of the first *Critique.*[14]

But Kant also gave a novel sense to the term "idealism" when he used it—along with the associated adjective "ideal" and the associated noun "ideality"—to designate his own "doctrinal concept" (*Lehrbegriff*) according to which the sensible forms of space and time, along with all that is intuited in accordance with those forms, has no "absolute," "objective" or "transcendental reality" as a "thing in itself," but possesses only "transcendental ideality" and has the status of an "appearance" (*Erscheinung*), formally conditioned by the universal but subjective forms of sensibility (space and time). While not being a mere "semblance" (*Schein*) and less yet an illusion (*Täuschung*), appearances in Kant have only "empirical reality" and are, strictly speaking, nothing but "representations in us."[15]

Kant's introduction of transcendental idealism transformed modern, mentalist idealism into an idealism of universal and necessary ("a priori") cognitive forms that shape all cognition and all objects of such cognition, ensuring the latter's reality within the limits of space and time, but negating any reality they might have outside and independent of those essentially subjective conditions.

Kant goes so far as to equate the "transcendental ideality" that marks space and time and the objects in space and time (appearances) with their outright nullity (*nichts*).[16] The reversal of fortunes for the term "idea" and its derivatives seems complete. Once, in Plato, the designation of what is most real and actually solely real, the late, modern descendants of Plato's "idea"—"idealism," "ideal" and "ideality"—denote and connote what is the least real to the point of being nothing rather than something at all.[17]

The extreme to which Kant's transcendental idealism had pushed the modern reevaluation of the ideal—from sole-being through being-in-us to being-nothing—provoked anti-idealist reactions on the part of his contemporary critics and critical successors. F. H. Jacobi coined the term "nihilism" (*Nihilismus*)[18] to unmask and denounce the implications of an idealism turned transcendental. He went on to oppose the alleged annihilating idealism of the Kantian philosophy with a dogmatic, transcendental realism centered around existence assertions and knowledge claims about the things in themselves that were supposedly based on the triple evidence of "feeling" (Gefühl), "faith" (*Glaube*) and "revelation" (*Offenbarung*). F. W. J. Schelling sought to counterbalance and complete the subjectivism of Kant's idealism, centered around the constitution of nature through the mind's transcendental forms and functions, with an objectivism and a realism that made the mind a constitutive part of an all-encompassing productive nature, thus joining idealist transcendental philosophy with a realist "philosophy of nature" (*Naturphilosophie*).

But the true turn in the development of idealism—a return of sorts to Plato's idealism—came with Hegel and his early introduction of a conception of mind or spirit as the sole basis and true nature of reality which did not draw on a modern, merely mentalist understanding of mind, as captured by the Latin word *mens*, but relied crucially on the ancient, specifically Platonic concept of the intellect (*nous*), devoid of the restriction to human psychology and suitably rendered through the more substantive term "spirit" (*Geist*) that suggest a measure of independence and self-sufficiency akin to that of the spiritual beings (*Geister*) of old. Like Plato before him, Hegel located true reality in "thought" (*Gedanke*) and "thinking" (*Denken*), again taking these terms not in their modern, mentalist meaning but as conveying the objectivity and necessity of logical entities or "concepts" (*Begriffe*) that are not so much in the mind as they are considered taking possession of the mind and advancing the latter from the merely mental to the substantially spiritual.

In order to render clear the anti-subjectivism of his ontology of thought determinations or "logic"—a logic not of forms only but also of content and of logically structured content at that—Hegel retrieves Plato's technical term "idea" from its mentalist reduction, restituting it to its original objectivist, even absolutist meaning. In particular, "idea" for Hegel marks the pre-disjunctive and post-differential, original unity of the ideal and the real—the unity of thought determinations not opposed to and alienated from reality and of a reality not external and foreign to thought determinations.[19]

On Hegel's understanding, the idea is not something ideal opposed to the real, something set out against the real as a merely ideal conceptual determination that reality lacks as much as it lacks reality. Rather the idea is what is most real about the real—what makes it into what it is and maintains it in this its being. For Hegel, the merely ideal and the merely real are but one-sided abstractions of a comprehensive totality that precedes the separation of the ideal and the real as their joint origin, as much as it succeeds the separation of the ideal and the real as their rejoined, intrinsically integrated ("concrete") reunification.

With all the renewed significance that the ancient term "idea" in its original Platonic understanding gained in Hegel's logico-ontological, "speculative" idealism, Hegel was not the first modern philosopher to return to the root meaning of Plato's ideas. Already Kant had supplemented his transcendental-idealist account of experience and its object domain—the world of sense—with an account of the conceptual space that lies beyond the realm of nature and its twofold limitation by the forms of space and time and by the pure concepts of the understanding ("categories"), along with the principles of possible experience based on them, chiefly among them the principle of causality.[20]

Yet ideas in Kant were concepts of objects that could not be known in their specific determinations and not even be known to exist, due to their conceptual location outside of the order of space and time and the restriction of (humanly) possible knowledge to the latter domain. For Kant the objects of ideas were objects of thought (*intelligibilia, Noumena*) to be entertained in pure thinking, as opposed to the objects of sense (*sensibilia, Phaenomena*) to be known by experience. While Kant maintained the functional need of such ideas for the ideal completion of experience,[21] and, more importantly, for the ideal direction and completion of morality through ideas such as that of virtue, of an afterlife and a supreme being,[22] he retained the general sense of ideas as unreal and counterfactual, even where—in matters of morality—they were meant to serve as the norms orienting and motivating human moral conduct under the central idea of freedom.

By contrast, Hegel vehemently opposes the only partial Platonism of Kant's critical account of the ideas that makes them more than mental and less than real. For Hegel, the idea involves the reality of the ideal as much as it implies the ideality of the real. Reality is only in thought and as thought—with thought being understood logically as well as ontologically. Conversely, thought as such is always already real as the logico-ontological formative content in all that is.

Moreover, unlike Kant and not unlike Plato, especially the later Plato for whom ideas are subject to processes of contradiction and change (dialectic), Hegel regards the idea and its material specifications, the thoughts, as subject to movement and to developmental movement at that.

But unlike in the Platonic precedent, in which the dialectical movement remains formal and abstractly relational, in Hegel the thought process that the idea undergoes in its logico-historical unfolding structurally describes a gradual, lawfully governed development from the inherent but latent presence of the idea ("in itself") to its full blown, completely explicit manifestation ("for itself").[23] It is a process that has its mental or rather spiritual manifestation in the progression from logical concepts through conceptions of nature to the emerging and ever more adequate self-consciousness of spirit as such. There is no counterpart in Plato to this logical history of mind or spirit and to the voyage of self-discovery and self-revelation in which the mind or spirit is involved in Hegel. With its systematic linkage of logical structure and logical development, of reason and history Hegel proves himself not a Platonist but a modernist, a participant in the modern endeavor to link development and structure, change and order, progress and preservation in a world marked by constant change under the twin appearance of the loss of the old and the opportunity for the new.

Reason and Reality

The developmental account of the unity-in-difference that is the idea in Hegel is primarily the idea's own logico-ontological development. In architectonic terms, the idea's progressive unfolding ranges from the idea being in itself, as presented in the conceptual sequence of categorical determinations in the Logic, through its being extraneous to itself (in the other), as detailed in the ontological account of the material world in the Philosophy of Nature, to its eventual and final return into itself, as featured in the conceptual history of the human world in the Philosophy of Spirit. The latter, final part and phase of the systematic developmental process of the idea again divides into three forms under which spirit appears as it is in itself and for itself in the world of human social relations and cultural productions: as spirit under the guise of individual consciousness and self-consciousness ("subjective spirit"); as spirit objectified in collections of human beings and their collective consciousness and self-consciousness ("objective spirit"); and as spirit manifesting itself as such in the cultural productions of art, religion and science, chiefly the super science of philosophy ("absolute spirit").[24]

Within the sphere of spirit—in particular, of objective spirit—the developmental nature of the idea, which in the logical and natural spheres is ostensibly ahistorical, takes on the outward form of human history. The historically manifest logical unfolding of objective spirit receives its systematic treatment in the philosophy of history, which presents the successive unfolding of self-differentiating spirit over the course of time and in a sequence of places. For Hegel history philosophically considered consists in spirit—under its objective guise as the "world spirit" (*Weltgeist*)—realizing itself progressively in a spatiotemporal sequence of cultures, each self-enclosed and limited to a specific period of history and a determinate region of the earth. In particular, Hegel contrasts and compares the cultures of the "oriental world," chiefly comprising India, Persia and China, the cultures of the "ancient world," essentially Greece and Rome, and the cultures of the "Germanic world," encompassing medieval and modern Europe.[25]

For Hegel Greek culture, including classical Athenian culture and Plato figuring in it, marks the middle point of the world-historical developmental process. Compared to the chronologically and logically prior Eastern world and its set of worldviews, it represents the step from the absolute rule of single leaders in large centralized states and empires ("oriental despotism")[26] to the self-rule of the people instituted in a multitude of largely independent city-states ("Greek freedom").[27] The key feature of the Greek culture and its worldview, as epitomized in fifth-century Athens, is the discovery—or rather the invention—of the human individual as an independent, "free" being existing in its own world, a world different both from the natural world and that of the Gods and a world largely of the individual's own design and making.[28]

According to Hegel, the main manifestation of the Greeks' inventive discovery of the newly free human individual is classical Greek art, chiefly human sculpture. But Hegel also includes among the advances brought about by the nascent individualism of Greek culture the political establishment of the Greek city-state (*polis*), characterized by popular rule ("democracy") and exhibiting the traits of a social sculpture in the manner of a political work of art.[29] Moreover, Hegel stresses the organic nature of the "democratic state," which is ruled not by the subjective, arbitrary will of a single individual but by the politically constituted will of the people or the "objective will."[30]

Yet when placed in a comprehensive, world-historical context, the Greek world, including Athens, exhibits not only advancement and expansion over and against the "oriental world" but also limitations and shortcomings in comparison with the world succeeding it—essentially the modern word. In particular, Hegel notes that the focus on the individual human being to be found in the ancient world is limited to a generalized and typified conception of individuality and lacks the inwardness ("subjectivity") characteristic of human individuality in the modern world. Hegel considers the latter advancement a cultural consequence of the Christian religion, especially of its modernist modification in Northern European Protestantism. By contrast, Hegel stresses the embeddedness of the classical Greek individual into a sociopolitical order that he portrays as severely limiting the free development of individuality through the social stricture of established customs, traditional *mores* and the reigning *ethos* of a culturally conditioned community.

But Hegel also finds in ancient Greece—more precisely, in classical Athens—the beginnings of a different kind of freedom, individual freedom, that was to be brought to full fruition only with the advent of Christianity and its long-term philosophical fallout, the modern moral and political worldview. According to Hegel, the Athenian beginnings of modern, individual freedom are ambivalent though.[31] They represent as much an enrichment as an impoverishment—the gain of greater personal freedom in people's intellectual and practical lives as well as the loss of communal ties that lent social support to people by providing their lives with overall direction and greater purpose.

On Hegel's balanced account of the cultural gains and losses involved in late classical Greece, the advantages and advancements involved in individual freedom are represented chiefly by the figure of Socrates.[32] For Hegel the intellectual and moral revolution brought about by Socrates largely consists in assigning personal responsibility to individual human beings for the views and values they hold and heed. In particular, Hegel cites Socrates's appeal to an inner moral voice (*daimonion*), akin in status and function to "conscience" (*Gewissen*) in the modern world,[33] as evidence for the world-historical move, initiated by Socrates, from collective customs and convictions to individually held beliefs and attitudes. Yet Hegel also acknowledges the disruptive, even dissolving effect that the introduction of individual responsibility into people's thinking and doing proved to have on communal life, especially on the life of the political community, for which the departure from established beliefs and engrained customs brought with it dissension and division.

However, according to Hegel, the real threat to social stability and to the political order was not posed by the Socratic revolution but by the contemporary populist enlightenment movement of the sophists, who introduced relativism and skepticism into the intellectual, social and civic lives of their students and followers.[34] In particular, Hegel contrasts the recourse to a reliable, even infallible inner voice guiding and ruling human conduct to be found in Socrates with the sophists' appeal to personal predilections and unstable pseudo-standards based on the variable evaluations resulting from the excessive exercise of "subjective freedom."[35] On Hegel's construal, Plato's republic is, to a large extent, a critical reaction—and an overreaction at that—to the sophistical pseudo-revolution in morals and politics.

Plato's Republic

Hegel's sympathetic portrayal and appreciative assessment of Plato's political philosophy focuses on two, seemingly diverging features of the philosopher's state as laid out in the *Republic*: the alleged chimerical character of Plato's republic as a mere figment of the philosophical mind removed from reality and useless in actual political life; and the polemical character of Plato's republic as an antidemocratic political institution fundamentally at odds with Athenian democracy. Against past and recent attempts to marginalize the *Republic* as a piece of idle speculation, Hegel insists on the constitutive task of philosophy to conceptually grasp actual political reality, rather than take recourse to dreaming up an ideal political order located in a remote location or a far away future. Hegel explicitly includes Plato among the political philosophers that face political reality and confront its challenges. Yet Hegel also credits Plato with a critique of the democratic state that seems to place Plato at odds with Athenian political reality and with the general task of philosophy to reconcile people with the realities of their actual lives.[36]

Hegel thus provides a puzzling twofold portrayal of Plato—as aiming at the reconstruction of political reality in line with philosophy's overall task of reconciling human beings with the reality in which they live, on the one hand, and as constructing a city-state fundamentally at variance with Athenian political reality, on the other hand. The tensions inherent in this double portrayal of Plato can be resolved by means of a philosophical distinction that is fundamental to Hegel's philosophy of history. For Hegel the reality to be ascertained and appreciated by philosophy in general and by political philosophy in particular is not the contingent reality of particular facts and events shaped by chance and circumstance. Rather Hegel engages in an evaluative understanding of (politico-historical) reality that purposively includes only what it is truly significant and historically or politically effective, as assessed in a philosophical perspective informed by the idealist restriction of the real to the conceptual or the rational.

On Hegel's understanding, that and only that is real in the philosophically relevant sense—actually real or "actual" (*wirklich*)—which is expressive of conceptual determinations to be identified and attributed by discriminating reason. The reverse equally holds for Hegel: what is established conceptually by philosophical reason also manifests itself in history and politics. In the famous double phrase from the Preface to Hegel's *Philosophy of Right*, "What is rational that is actual; and what is actual that is rational."[37]

Hegel's daring double identification of the rational with the actual and of the actual with the rational dissociates practical philosophy, including political philosophy, from an idealism that opposes the idea to its always only imperfect expression or instantiation. Rather than subjecting the idea to the status of an absolute standard, always to be aimed at and never to be attained, Hegel considers the idea to be what is effective—and to that extent actual—in historical or political reality and what thereby constitutes the conceptual core and the rational character of that very reality.

Hegel's dissociation of the idea from its status as a perpetual "ought" (*Sollen*), forever frustrated by the "is" of reality—the latter being the normatively idealist reading of Plato advanced by Kant[38]—seeks to return the idea to its pre-Kantian, genuinely Platonic meaning as that which is most real in all there is and which, moreover, is itself of the nature of thought. Accordingly, the task of philosophy in general and of political philosophy in particular is to exhibit the presence of reason in a given (historical or political) reality by showing that reality to express adequately if not conclusively a rational order of things.

Applied to Hegel, Plato's rational justification of reality allows an anti-idealist, outright realist reading of the *Republic*, according to which Plato's work does not present a counterimage different from and even opposed to actual political reality but exhibits the conceptual deep structure of the state—more precisely, the Greek city-state (*polis*)—as such. In seemingly speaking about a state unlike the ones inhabited by real people in real time, Plato is seen by Hegel as describing the innermost workings of the *polis* as such, under abstraction from what is contingently and circumstantially deficient or defective about the political order in which the contemporary Greeks in general and Plato's Athenian fellow citizens in particular might have found themselves living.

Hegel goes so far as to apply his realist idealism or idealist realism about political ideas and ideas in politics to Plato's famous *dictum* about the political need for rulers to become philosophers and for philosophers to become rulers. Hegel shares neither the conventional construal of Plato's postulate as a call for the political empowerment of thinkers nor the dismissal of the called-for political rule of philosophers as a mere power fantasy on the part of ineffective intellectuals. On Hegel's reading, the convergence of philosophy and politics envisioned in the *Republic* conveys the merging of reason and reality—of the ideal and the real—in a state true to its conceptual nature as a political order marked by the rule of justice in its constituent parts as well as in the whole.[39] For Hegel the growing together of philosophy and politics, as represented in a figurative way by Plato's personalizing talk of rulers and philosophers turning into each other, is not some sudden turn of events to be hoped for in the future but expressive of the actual constitution of the just state as such. Plato's republic, rather than being the state "in the idea" (Kant), is, so Hegel, the state in actual reality—the state conceived in terms of its rational essence.

According to Hegel, the reality actually contained in Plato's republic is the actuality of the Greek state itself, which consists in the public manifestation of the established and ingrained Greek sociopolitical *mores* or of "Greek ethical life" (*griechische Sittlichkeit*).[40] Hegel's reading of Plato the political philosopher is based on the meta-philosophical view that any philosophy is its time cast in thought. Therefore the peculiar task and the specific accomplishment of the philosophers, including political philosophers, cannot be to transcend their own time and to assume an imaginary or utopian standpoint elsewhere or, for that matter, nowhere. Instead philosophy, including political philosophy, is to provide conceptual articulation and rational expression to what is already actual, be it ancient Athens or modern Europe.[41]

Still Hegel finds fault with the ways in which Plato, while not evading his own times—as a superficial and false reading of the *Republic* would have it—represents the essence of actual Greek political theory and practice. For one, Hegel sees Plato as portraying the essence of the Greek state at a moment in Greek political history, in the aftermath of the Peloponnesian War, when the *ethos* of the *polis* is no longer truly in evidence and in effect. According to Hegel, by the time of Plato the formerly coherent and cogent ethical character of civic life in the city-state already is in dissolution, giving way to manifest traits of increasing individualism and growing tendencies toward fragmentation and particularization.

On Hegel's account, Plato reacts to those contemporary tendencies with the aggressive portrayal of an already vanished Greece and its political ethos of social solidarity and political stability. On Hegel's assessment then, Plato is to be faulted not for an escape into an imaginary and ideal political world but for a nostalgic return to a recently real world. But rather than to engage, as he did, in reactionary politics and restorative political theory—a philosophical politics of responding to recent changes by ignoring or maligning them—it would have behooved Plato, as any philosopher, so Hegel, to extract the rational core and conceptual content in or behind the manifest changes in Greek political life that were occurring or already had occurred in Plato's time. As an instance of those changes, Hegel cites, in addition to the loss of social solidarity and political stability, the gains in freedom—in individual, personal freedom—that came with the gradual dissolution of the previously reigning Greek sociopolitical *ethos*.

Hegel refers specifically to Pericles's persuasive portrayal of Athenian liberal democracy and cultured urbanity in his funeral oration for the war dead at the end of the first year's campaigns of the Peloponnesian War, as recorded—or rather re-created—

by Thucydides.[42] For Hegel the positive elements of the Athenian democratic developments anticipate, albeit on a small scale and in imperfect execution, the kind of freedom—personal and extensive—to be introduced on a world-historical scale by the religious revolution of Christianity and its cultural aftermath with their ethico-political standards of individual morality and freedom of conscience.

By focusing exclusively on the ailments of Athenian (proto-) modernity and studiously ignoring the latter's liberating potential, Plato—on Hegel's reading of the *Republic*—erred in a direction entirely unsuspected and undetected by all those who have charged Plato with being too much of an idealist about political possibilities. For Hegel Plato in the *Republic* is not too idealist but insufficiently so in that he failed to realize and recognize the role that "subjective freedom" was playing already in the late classical world and that such freedom was to play in a world no longer ancient and traditionalist—in the modern world, as portrayed in Hegel's own political philosophy and its judicious assessment of the modern state.[43]

Hegel's State

In the *Philosophy of Right*, published in 1821 as a manual for his lecture courses on "natural law and political science" (*Naturrecht und Staatswissenschaft*)[44] at the University of Berlin, Hegel undertook himself what he had found lacking in Plato's political philosophy—lending conceptual clarity and rational reconstruction to the actually existing state of his time. In Hegel's case the actual state to be assessed and appreciated in its rational dignity was the modern territorial state that had emerged in Europe during the seventeenth and eighteenth centuries, marked by international sovereignty without, the rule of law within, a monarchical constitution, a bureaucracy of appointed state officials, the institution and inclusion of legislative bodies and a complex social stratification based on status and possessions.

For Hegel the chief world-historical feature of the actual modern state—of the state as conceived and conceptualized by Hegel, in short, Hegel's state—is the latter's political power to grant and guarantee its citizens freedom—more precisely, personal, individual, "subjective" freedom. Hegel's modern state provides the formative framework in which and due to which individuals first are able to pursue their own ends in a safe and supportive political condition and to lead lives significantly shaped both by their personal preferences and by their public, civic obligations.[45]

According to Hegel, the modern state not simply enables the exercise of "subjective freedom," as though that freedom were a natural good antedating the state's concern with it. For Hegel the state first renders human beings free in the relevant sense by making them evolve and enhance their natural abilities in a sociocivic context marked by coexistence and cooperation as much as by competition and conflict. In the process, individuals are turned into citizens. As citizens human beings become structurally integrated but independently functioning parts, or "members,"[46] of an organic whole—the political community or the state—that would not be whole without them, just as they would not be fully functioning without the whole.

Hegel's modern state is neither the liberal state of modern times that minimally and negatively safeguards prepolitically given, "natural" rights nor the premodern state that subjects human beings to traditionally given societal structures and strictures. Unlike the liberal state, Hegel's state is chiefly concerned with the enhancement and advancement of its citizens' lives, which would be different lives, simpler and easier perhaps but also less significant and less "free," were it not for the state's challenging demands on its citizens to cultivate an individuality that is at once personally chosen and civically responsible.

Hegel presents a threefold articulation of the comprehensive formative framework that is the modern state: the juridical basis for social interaction provided by formal legal rules under the guise of "abstract right" (*abstractes Recht*),[47] the moral foundation of individual action by the rigid regulation of intentions and motives through "morality" (*Moralität*)[48] and the comprehensive orientation and motivation of civico-social existence by contentually concrete and effectively engrained standard practices of living with each other and living together, termed "ethical life" (*Sittlichkeit*).[49]

The specific modernity of Hegel's state—a modernity that distinguishes it both from the traditional, premodern and from the liberal, alternatively modern state—resides chiefly in its novel conception of "ethical life," a designation that harks back to the function, though not to the substance, of premodern *ethos* or "customs" (in German, *Sitten*), which previously held together societies and states by respected rules that had assumed the status and function of a "second nature." By contrast, modern ethical life includes the quintessentially modern regard and concern for the individuals in their own, independent worth ("dignity"), distinct from the standardizing influence of societal norms and regulations.

For Hegel the "ethical life" of modernity, as shaped and secured by the modern state, operates at three distinct but interacting levels. Modern ethical life has its natural or quasi-natural basis in the reproductive unity of the "family" (*Familie*),[50] receives its sociocultural development in the sphere of commerce and consumption or in "civil society" (*bürgerliche Gesellschaft*)[51] and culminates in the sociopolitical unity of the citizenry that is the state (*Staat*),[52] more precisely the state in its narrowly political sense or the "political state" (*politischer Staat*).[53]

On Hegel's construal, the state as the supreme political entity, while regulating the social institutions of the family and civil society, has its own ultimate purpose in the political arena as such—by establishing and safeguarding the constitutional division and cooperation between the political powers within (legislative, executive and judicative) and ensuring rightful international relations between individual states. Hegel's political state is, ideally, a state of peace that maintains rightful relations within and without to allow the free flourishing of its citizenry.

To be sure, Hegel argues for a constitutional monarchy with a hereditary figurehead symbolizing the political unity of the modern state in a single individual.[54] Still the formative function of the state in the making and the shaping of its citizens and the integration of individual pursuits at the level of the family and civil society into the political unity of the state links Hegel's monarchically constituted state to the republican tradition. In particular, Hegel stresses the need to cultivate the political mentality and the civic attitude of the citizenry (*politische Gesinnung, Patriotismus*).[55] But unlike the civically geared republicanism of early modern political theory and practice, which he regards as having made citizens' lives substantially subservient to the republican state, Hegel has the high modern state grant its citizens a twofold existence—one private and personal devoted to individual pursuits and one public and civic dedicated to service to the political community that is the state, effectively linking substantial and subjective, political and personal freedom.

Looking back to Plato, Hegel remarks on the sharp distinctions that separates his monarchically constituted and republican minded state from the former's ideal-real republic. By effectively eliminating marriage, private property and free choice of profession, Plato's republic lacks the functionally independent spheres of the family and civil society and proves inimical to the personal freedom characteristic of the modern era in general and to its political manifestation in the modern state in particular.[56] On Hegel's understanding, the illiberal traits of Plato's republic are continuous with the generally limited conception of freedom in classical Greece, where political freedom is restricted to full citizens and personal freedom curtailed in the interest of political freedom.[57]

There is one aspect, though, in which Plato's republic and Hegel's state seem in agreement: in the antidemocratic bent that makes both of them exclude the populace, or large parts of it, from direct political influence and specifically from political freedom.[58] The conviction common to Plato and Hegel that rule and government are to be based on expertise and appointment rather than on popular representation and general election is quite at variance with the republican tradition of self-rule. Yet Plato and Hegel retain their basic allegiance to another core characteristic of classical republicanism—the equitable rule of laws, as opposed to the arbitrary "rule of men." Subsequent to the *Republic*, Plato devoted an entire late work, *The Laws* (*Nomoi*), to the giving and enacting of laws in what he described as the "second-best" republic,[59] one more real yet than the earlier, ideal-real republic of the eponymous work and perhaps closer yet to Hegel's much later concern with the actual state and its realization through public legislation.

4

The People's Republic: Fichte and Plato

> "Man, when perfected, is the best of animals;
> but if he be isolated from law and justice
> he is the worst of all."[1]

An Inner Platonism

To place Fichte's political philosophy in general and his political republicanism in particular in relation to Plato's thinking about the nature, structure and function of the ideal constitution of the city-state (*politeia*) is not merely an antiquarian exercise in philosophical comparison through comparative philosophy. In many regards Plato forms the intellectual and spiritual horizon for Fichte's overall philosophy and its dramatic development, which is as much a development out of Kant, as it is a development away from Kant. Still it would be an exaggeration to make Fichte's move beyond Kant a return to Plato. Even as a Platonist of sorts,[2] Fichte remains a Kantian, profoundly and continuously committed to Kant's innovative insistence on the spontaneity and freedom of the human mind. In Kant as well as Fichte, this is a spontaneity in theoretical matters and a freedom in practical matters that has the mind's cognitive and conative faculty ("reason") not be dependent on an independently given, absolute order of things but exercise its autonomous legislation in establishing and enacting the interdependent lawful orders of nature and freedom.[3]

While not being an overt and explicit feature of his philosophical thought, Fichte's Platonism is a matter of the overall orientation of his philosophy. The latter aims beyond experience at its ground and basis in what cannot be experienced but without which experience itself would not be possible in the first place. Kant had introduced the sum total of the nonempirical conditions of everything empirical under the traditional but virtually obsolete term "transcendental." His reuse of the term had suggested a continuity of sorts between the universal ontological predicates of old—chiefly the one, the true, the good ("*unum, verum, bonum*")—and the newly identified constitutive features underlying any experience and its objects, those formative factors being space, time and the categories.[4]

But Kant had remained largely silent about the ontological status of the nonempirical, transcendental conditions of the empirical, treating them as presuppositions for something else rather than as entities in their own right. In addition to introducing space and time as the sensible forms for the intuition of empirical entities ("appearances"), he had allowed for the objective representation of the form of outer intuition as an intuition in its own right, terming it "formal intuition" (*formale Anschauung*), and had granted to space and time each the status of an "imaginary being" (*ens imaginarium*).[5] In introducing the categories as the intellectual forms for the thinking of objects, he had relegated them to mere "forms of thought" (*Gedankenformen*)[6] devoid of content and meaning, safe for their necessary relation to the spatiotemporal features of objects that at once realize and restrict the existential import of the categories.

Eager to continue and complete the Kantian revolution in theoretical philosophy, Fichte sets out to further define the status of the transcendental dimension beyond its functional role of first enabling experience, along with the objects of experience, previously assigned to it by Kant. More specifically, Fichte seeks to identify the inner nature and intrinsic being of the conditioning structure underlying the natural order of the empirical world. In so doing, he addresses and treats the transcendental conditions as a domain of its own with a type of being deemed more fundamental than that of empirical things. Fichte's post-Kantian reflexive turn toward the transcendental domain as such involves an epistemology and ontology of the transcendental that adduces extraordinary cognitive resources, such as "intellectual intuition," for identifying and characterizing the extraordinary domain outside of experience that conditions experience along with the objects of experience ("nature").

Notoriously, Fichte equates the transcendental domain with the "I" (*Ich*), or the "pure I" (*reines Ich*), to be precise. In so doing, he utilizes the nominalized first person pronoun to uniquely single out the dynamical core structure of human subjectivity that is essentially active and nothing but active, and self-active or spontaneously active at that.[7] Most importantly, though, Fichte's egological characterization of transcendental subjectivity draws on the self-reverting structure of the I—its constitutive feature of being-for-itself and being so both originally and persistently, as the pure form of self-consciousness that enables and informs all other consciousness of persons and objects.[8]

In order to avoid the facile confusion of the I transcendentally conceived—the generic or pure I as the pre- or proto-conscious condition of all consciousness—with the empirical, individuated I of a particular human being, Fichte soon substitutes the first-person characterization of the transcendental domain with less psychologically connoted conceptions, including the recourse to the first person plural "We" (*Wir*)[9] and to its third-person neutral characterization as "absolute knowledge" (*absolutes Wissen*)[10] or "the absolute" (*das Absolute*),[11] the latter term referring—in the first instance—not to some supranatural, divine entity but to all that which is absolute or unconditioned in human knowledge, regardless of the particulars of the latter's bearer and the latter's object.[12]

In epistemological terms, Fichte characterizes the transcendental I and its functional successors with terms and concepts that were, or would have been, emphatically repudiated by Kant's critical account of the grounds and bounds of human knowledge. Specifically, Fichte considers pure I-hood to be the object of cognition of an actual nonsensory, "intellectual intuition" (*intellektuelle Anschauung*),[13] granting it the status of a "fact-act" (*Tathandlung*)[14] specifically different from the "facts" (*Tatsachen*) of consciousness, a difference due to the former's self-referential and self-productive character as spontaneous self-reverting subjectivity. Moreover, Fichte widens the epistemology and ontology of transcendental subjectivity to encompass an entire world of beings unassailable by the senses but to be brought forth by the intellect, in the process constituting a world of the understanding and its mind-borne or "noumenal" objects (*Noumena*), structurally analogous but contentually superior to the world of the senses and its apparential or phenomenal objects (*Phaenomena*).

To be sure, Fichte's egological conception of transcendental subjectivity harks back to Kant's account of transcendental apperception and to the essential virtual presence of the basic thought form "I think" (*ich denke*) in all possible consciousness.[15] But what in Kant is only the empty generic form of thought requiring a twofold saturation through the specific intellectual forms of the categories and the specific sensible form of time (and, by extension, of space), in Fichte becomes a domain of its own, to be explored by a novel transcendental science, the "Science of Knowledge" or "Doctrine of Science" (*Wissenschaftslehre*),[16] and considered more actual and effective in its ideal, noumenal or thought status than the empirical reality of the phenomenal objects.

It is this noumenalism[17]—the theoretical conviction of and the practical commitment to the primacy of thinking over sensing and the superiority of the ideal over the real—that links Fichte, across the great divide between the ancients and the moderns, back to Plato and to the latter's insistence on the exclusive reality of thought, the merely apparent reality of the empirical world and the human calling to transcend, in one's essential efforts at knowledge and action, the mere semblance of being in favor of being itself and to leave behind fleeting sensation in favor of pure thought.

To be sure, Kant had already resorted to Plato when enlarging his critical epistemology of intuitional forms (space and time) and pure concepts of the understanding (categories) with "concepts of reason" or "ideas" (*Ideen*), explicitly taking the latter term from Plato and appropriating it for the designation of objects that, in principle, elude experience and are expressive of the unconditional in human knowledge.[18] But Kant's transcendental ideas (the soul, the world, God) remained regulative, serving as the ideal focal points for infinitely enlarged and extended experience rather than as constitutive concepts for first enabling objects and their cognition, as in Plato. Viewed from Kant's perspective, Plato had uncritically assimilated (regulative) ideas to (constitutive) categories, in effect confusing categorical concepts, which find their instantiation in the very experience they constitute, with ideal concepts, which do not find their adequate expression in any experience, but instead lead human thinking and doing beyond experience toward an ideal, perfect order erected in sheer thought and in utter abstraction from things finite and imperfect.

Moreover, the constitutive role granted to practical ideas, chiefly the idea of freedom, in Kant's moral philosophy did not involve the constitution of experience and its objects but the determination of the will for the purpose of morality and the ideal formation of the complete object of moral willing, that is, the highest good. Most importantly, though, Kant had based the reality of the practical idea of freedom and the associated ideas of a personal afterlife and a personal God not on genuine knowledge to be obtained by purely intellectual insight, but on the alternative surrogate epistemic resources of feeling (*Gefühl*) and faith (*Glaube*).[19] More specifically, he had rejected the possibility of any theoretical cognition, be it immediate or inferential, of the possibility and actuality of moral freedom, divine moral arbitration and psychic immortality.

Fichte in turn undertakes a reevaluation of the real-ideal distinction maintained by Kant. He assigns ontic and epistemic priority to the ideal and turns the latter into the truly real, while relegating the formerly real to the status of a mere semblance. For Fichte, it is thinking and its realization in willing that are of foremost reality in human life. According to Fichte, human beings are, in the first instance, spontaneous thinkers and free actors that constitute the natural and spiritual world through their thinking and willing. Structurally speaking, Fichte transposes Kant's transcendental idealism of mind-constituted experience to an idealism of self-determined willing and its self-constituted moral order. Rather than having human beings shape and change the world in which they live to conform ever more but never enough to the ideal requirements of reason and its prime condition—freedom—Fichte makes the world inhabited by human beings the imperfect manifestation of an ideal moral order in which individuality and imperfection are always already superseded by absolute unity and utter identity.

The latent, inner Platonism of Fichte's philosophy manifests itself with increased intensity over the extended course of its development, which involves not so much discontinuities and reversals as rearticulations and reemphases applied to the core project of vindicating infinite freedom to finite human existence. Throughout, Fichte's philosophy is marked by an *élan*—his own preferred terms being "striving" (*Streben*)[20] and "longing" (*Sehnen*)[21]—beyond limitations of all kinds, borne by an elemental existential certainty of the human "vocation" or "destination" (*Bestimmung*) to infinite perfection as much as by the realistic realization of the lack and failure bound up with the human condition.[22]

Another Platonic feature, in addition to the speculative eroticism expressive of lack and longing that animates and advances Fichte's philosophical thinking is the language and conceptuality of "appearance" (*Erscheinung*).[23] Fichte draws on this originally Platonic term (*phainomenon*) in his middle years, after abandoning the overtly egological presentation of transcendental subjectivity. The recourse to the term and concept is intended to designate the elusive and ideal presence of the unconditional, the infinite or the absolute in finite human existence, where it "appears" under the twin guise of (absolute) cognition and (pure) volition. For Fichte, human existence epitomized by theoretically grounded and practically relevant "knowledge" (*Wissen*) is at once the appearance of the *absolute,* the latter lending soul and substance to human finitude, and the *appearance* of the absolute, the former expressing the lack of completeness and the absence of perfection on the part of finite existence.

A particularly striking feature of Fichte's inner Platonism is his later recourse to the Platonic conception of universal forms. In a daring divergence from current usage, he employs the German term *Gesicht*[24] to convey the visual connotation and the optical etymology of Plato's technical terms *idea* and *eidos*, both in turned derived from the Greek root for "seeing." While the German word *Gesicht* usually means "face" corresponding to the Latin *facies*, Fichte draws on the noun's original linguistic status as the nominalized past perfect participle of "seeing" (*sehen*), to signify "that which is seen."[25] Today, the Latin past participle *visum*, literally meaning "what is seen," is still used in German, as well as in other European languages, for a "visual record" (*Sichtvermerk*) that is entered into a travel document.

Arguably, the hidden Platonic heritage in Fichte's philosophical manner even extends to his inventive and imaginative use of images designed and deployed to convey highly abstract concepts and lines of thought that are removed from illustration and example by way of striking images and captivating notions. This holds especially for the psycho- and theomorphic casting of much of Fichte's later philosophical work, which draws on human psychology and Christian theology to address the nature of the absolute. Instances of such a philosophical mythology in the later Fichte are the portrayal of the step from the absolute itself to its manifestation under conditions of finitude as the former's "revelation" (*Offenbarung*), and the interpretation of the appearance of the absolute as being based on the latter's "drive" (*Trieb*) to manifest as itself outside of itself.[26]

In fact, the entire Fichtean project of explicating the status and function of transcendental subjectivity in essentially dynamic, developmental terms along the lines of a "pragmatic history of the human mind,"[27] which proved inspirational and influential for Schelling's and Hegel's subsequent phenomenological accounts of mind and matter, is akin in status and function to the tall tales told in Plato's dialogues for pedagogical or political purposes. Dramatizing and, as it were, historicizing transcendental subjectivity by means of the presentational device of a "story"—the latter being the other meaning of the German word for "history" (*Geschichte*), drawn upon by Fichte himself to convey the fabricated status of the transcendental master myth or fiction (*Fiktion*)[28]—serves to render in familiar and comprehensible terms what is in itself conceptually situated outside of place and time and is itself not temporally extended but of the nature of instantaneous transtemporality.

To be sure, significant differences in method and doctrine remain and prevail between Plato and Fichte, which make Fichte at once less and more than a Platonist—less so due to his continued commitment to a Kantian critical thinking that eschews exalted claims to extraordinary insight, and more so in terms of Fichte's considerable originality in combining Kantian sobriety with Platonic *pathos*. As Fichte himself notes when confronting the work of ancient and more recent, modern Platonists and neo-Platonists: "*Platonist*:—I believe myself to be more."[29]

Citizens and Human Beings

The inner Platonism of Fichte's post-Kantian philosophy also permeates significant parts of his political philosophy. To begin with, Fichte's public intellectual personality as an eminently political philosopher whose published works trace and follow the theoretical and practical challenges posed by the contemporary events of the French Revolution, the Napoleonic Wars and the Liberation Wars, recalls Plato's theoretical immersion and practical involvement in things political, from the failed Sicilian venture—or rather, adventure—to the fictitious founding of the ideal city-state (*The Republic*) and its second-best surrogate (*The Laws*) to the attempted definition of the politician or statesman (*The Statesman*) as a life form rivaling with that of the philosopher and the latter's deficient double, the pseudo-philosopher (*The Sophist*).

Fichte also shares with Plato the integration of political philosophy into the larger whole of philosophy, the latter conceived as a supreme science (*episteme, Wissenschaft*) bent on genuine knowledge, as opposed to semblance and illusion, and on knowledge of what is best and brightest—in Plato's phrase, the sun-like, intrinsic and independent good itself.[30] Moreover, Plato and Fichte are akin in the radical, life-changing, outright revolutionary import and impact they attribute to philosophy in general and to its political potential in particular.[31] Doctrinal differences notwithstanding, both Plato and Fichte envision and aim at a radical departure from the quotidian comforts of established traditions and engrained opinions in favor of a life led on the basis and by the lights of superior insight into the constitution of natural and social reality.

To be sure, Plato and Fichte, akin as they might seem in politico-philosophical attitude and demeanor, remain separated from each other by the great gulf that divides the ancients and the moderns in general and that keeps apart Kantian and Platonic idealism in particular. Neither the focus on freedom nor the conceptually connected centrality of the will so prominent, even primary, in Kant and Fichte are to found in Plato, who remains committed to a comprehensive cosmology that integrates human existence into a unitary natural-supranatural order of things governed throughout by fixed principles (Forms) and removed from the essentially modern conception of free individual and social human self-development, in turned based on the theoretically ensured possibility of cosmological freedom and its practical realization as human freedom.

The distinctive feature of modern human beings as free beings under laws of their own rational nature, which makes them "ends in themselves" and subjects of unconditional, "natural" rights as well as duties, also informs the understanding of political life to be found in Fichte. As free beings, human beings are not first and foremost citizens of a particular polity, however ideal or perfect, but world citizens, whose cosmopolitan existence as members of a world composed entirely of any and all such free beings precedes, conjoins and succeeds any narrowly political association. In Fichte—as in most modern thinkers—human beings, while being originally free in a radical and practical sense, only subsequently become citizens, and they become so under the enabling as well as restrictive conditions of civic socialization that in turn are, or are to be, informed by the extracivic and prepolitical, "natural" status of freedom.

A further feature that separates Fichte from Plato is the clear distinction between ethics and politics that all but rescinds the substantial analogy introduced by Plato between the soul and the city,[32] and their formally as well as materially similar orders defined by relations of justice between its constituent elements or component "parts."[33] For Fichte, as for most moderns philosophizing under the influence of ethico-religious pluralization and fragmentation, political life is basically distinct from the ethical life form, involving a freedom of its own ("personal freedom") and following its own laws, even as the latter might formally resemble the rules specific to the moral or ethical conduct that is based on moral or ethical freedom and its law.

In his modernist separation between juridical law—or "right" (*Recht*)—and moral or ethical law (*Moral, Ethik*)—Fichte even exceeds Kant's distinction of the two spheres of the legislation of freedom: the inner, ethical legislation concerning the motivational basis of action in principled intentions ("maxims") and the outer, juridical legislation limited to the restrictive regulation of the outward manifestation of the free exercise of "choice" (*Willkür*). While stressing the principal exclusion of ethical conduct from juridical censorial control, Kant still sought to unite the two specifically different basic legislative modes of reason—law and ethics—in a unitary conception of human agency under one and the same (practical) reason, with each of the specifically different legislations involving unconditional obligation (categorical imperative) along with the latter's differentiation into materially specific laws ("metaphysical first principles") of right and virtue, respectively.[34]

As a consequence of their disagreement about the moral or extramoral basis of juridical law, Kant and Fichte differ in their assessment of the grounds for entering into, for remaining within and for leaving behind the specifically political association (under the rule of law) that is the state. For Kant the state of nature, while not necessarily being a state of vital endangerment to be left behind for reasons of survival and security as in Hobbes, is a state of legal endangerment in which the prepolitically given lawful status of free agency regulated by "natural law" (*Naturrecht*) is not protected from contingent competing claims and factual infringements. Accordingly, Kant regards it as a matter of unconditional, "moral" necessity to leave behind the state of nature, which, to be sure, does not lack laws and even possesses its own original, "natural" law, but lacks the means to ensure the publically effective rule of (natural) law. The civil state for which the naturally right but factually unjust state of nature is to be left behind is explicitly established and purposively designed to protect everyone's potentially conflicting prepolitical, natural rights with juridico-political means. The latter goal is achieved under the form of publically administered law ("public law"; *öffentliches Recht*), chiefly by the law governing the body politic as such ("state law"; *Staatsrecht*).[35]

For Fichte, by contrast, the abandonment of the state of nature and the adoption of the civil condition (*bürgerlicher Zustand*) under the guise of the civil state (*Staat*) and its juridico-political apparatus is a matter of choice, albeit one governed by prudential reason and hence amounting to a pragmatic necessity. More specifically, Fichte distinguishes between, on the one hand, the strict necessity on the part of every evolving human being of entering into initial basic social relations that first call forth the dormant potential for rational thought and action and, on the other hand, the subsequent and continuous engagement in reciprocal social relations of "mutual" and "reciprocal recognition" (*gegenseitige Anerkennung, wechselseitige Anerkennung*)[36] ruled by juridical law and its institutional condition—the state, primarily defined as a state of law and right.[37]

In making sociality a condition of the very possibility of rational self-consciousness, Fichte transforms the specifically moral necessity of entering into juridico-civic life, defended by Kant, into the ineluctable, "transcendental" requirement for intelligent practical existence to adopt a social life form. At the same time he replaces what in Kant had been a narrowly moral requirement to move from the generic social life form to a specifically civic and political existence, with an argument based on prudential reason and tied to a self-perfectionist conception of human social existence that includes civico-juridical advancement as a prerequisite for further forms of socially based human self-cultivation.

For Kant, the move from the state of nature to the civil state had been a matter of first enabling the realization of freedom in the external exercise of arbitrary choice. Freedom had to be considered fragile and tenuous, even under the best of circumstances, in a prepolitical state—the state of nature—that was lacking the juridico-political institution of public justice. Accordingly, for Kant the establishment of civil society or the state was a matter of practical necessity and moral obligation. From a juridico-moral perspective, the state in Kant is an unconditional end, because only the civil state makes possible the ameliorative transformation of unruly, unsocial or "wild" freedom into ruled, sociable or "well-ordered" freedom. By contrast, for Fichte the state arises as and remains a means to an end—a probate means, to be sure, but still an eligible means subject to prudential considerations of its institution and constitution.[38]

Fichte's pragmatic, instrumental and for that matter eminently political understanding of the state has important implications for the state's status and stability as the provider of law and right. For Kant, the moral origin of the state and its nature as the necessary condition of actual external freedom implied the latter's moral irresistibility. There could be no (legal) right to actively resist a juridico-political order that as such possessed moral sanction, regardless of any deficiencies of its actual operation due to its particular realization under the fallible conditions of political life. For Kant, political change, including improvements in the public administration of justice, was to take place not by revolt or revolution but by reform—and by reform "from above," through intelligent and insightful rulers ("enlightened princes"), at that.[39]

For Fichte, by contrast, the state is not an inviolable moral institution but a contingent historical artifice that presupposes the transcendental "history of self-consciousness" and that extends the latter's original accomplishment of free sociality into the public sphere of law and order constitutive of real, political history. The social contract, which in Kant had figured as the guiding principle ("idea") for articulating the (fictitious) popular legitimation of political rule, assumes the role of a contingent condition in Fichte. More specifically, the social contract is the subject of negotiation, revision and revocation in the manner of private contracts and unfolds into an entire architecture of social subcontracts. Chiefly among those further contracts is the "contract of subjection" (*Unterwerfungsvertrag*),[40] by means of which the constituent parts of an emerging civic association subject themselves freely to the power and authority of the state that is so being constituted.

In particular, Fichte argues for the right on the part of individuals that find themselves disadvantaged by the terms of a given social contract to cancel the existing contract and leave the compact, effectively giving up their rights as well as obligations, typically to exchange the old contract for a new one more favorable or just to their reasonable concerns and legitimate interests. While Fichte is well aware of the destabilizing implications of severable social contractual regulations, he seems to have regarded the principal permissibility and practical possibility of profound political change as an effective incentive for juridical and political improvements on the part of rulers, who are well advised to embrace reforms rather than repression when faced with the direct or indirect threat of revolution or revolt.[41]

Yet Fichte also insists that the improvements and adjustments to be extracted from the ruling forces presuppose the intellectual fitness and moral suitability ("worthiness") of the larger populace for an enhanced share in political life. Moreover, Fichte's vision for civic advancement and political liberalization involves not so much widespread, "democratic" participation in legislative matters and executive affairs (political freedom), as the politically guaranteed assurance of the rule of law and the publically furnished protection of individuals from unwarranted private and public interference (personal and civic freedom). The focus on a civically educated citizenry obediently appreciative of the rule of law lends to Fichte's state the double traits of a state of public right and of public education, effectively linking it back both to Plato's idea of a politico-pedagogical republic and to the latter's Roman and neo-Roman successor conceptions of a polity based on civic education and public service.

The State and the Nation

In Fichte's political philosophy, the basic republican character of the state as a state of public right and a state of civic education goes together with the distinctly modern, "liberal" elements chiefly manifest in his earlier works, which were developed in immediate engagement both with the French Revolution and the continuing Continental European tradition of natural law. In Fichte's peculiar political blending of individualistically liberal and civically republican features, the juridically ensured external freedom of civically constituted individuals is not treated as a political end in itself. Rather Fichte has the naturally free human beings who have transformed themselves into juridically free citizens undergo political forms of control and civic norms of conduct that are to serve and enhance the common good, instead of merely serving the interests of particular individuals or their combined collectivity.

As a result of the educative, formative and interventionist role of the state in the lives of its formally free citizens, Fichte's state, while remaining basically committed to natural law and its actualization under the rule of positive law and political right, takes on the features of an absolutist body politic. To be sure, on Fichte's understanding the state's claim and influence on its citizens lives is based not on the arbitrary exercise of political power but on claimed superior insight and is supposedly borne by the best of intentions. Again the similarity with Plato's expertocracy is apparent, even if Fichte does not seek to vindicate the power of politics to political philosophers.[42]

The illiberal implications, or rather dimensions, of Fichte's Platonic republicanism first come to the foreground in his political economy. As an appendix to his previously presented philosophy of law and an exercise in "applied politics," Fichte designs and demands the "closed commercial state."[43] By severing the state's trade ties to other states, Fichte seeks to ensure the political independence ("freedom") of the state. To that end he has the state close its borders to commercial trade and even to its citizens' travel and limit economic activity to its territorial confines. Moreover, the deinternationalization of commerce is accompanied by the nationalization of the economy. The state is to assume oversight over the national economy by fixing prices, closely monitoring the exchange of goods and instituting a restrictive monetary policy. While the interventionist and directional economico-political measures envisioned by Fichte are undertaken in the interest and for the purpose of political freedom, they involve a far-reaching infringement on the citizens' personal and civic freedom in business dealings and commercial transactions and, at least indirectly, in their entire private lives.

In a further extension of his politico-philosophical program of economic nationalization Fichte subjects the citizens of his state to educational nationalization by means of a civic educational system.[44] Here, too, the affinity between Fichte's and Plato's political pedagogy is apparent. By removing the children from parental educational control, the future citizens are subject to a formation that reflects civic concerns rather than private preferences. Fichte himself acknowledges the structural similarity of his plans and proposals for civic and public rather than domestic and private education to Plato's advocacy of abolishing the nuclear family. In a further analogy to the sociocultural revolution envisioned by Plato, Fichte seeks to remove intergenerational class barriers by extending public education to all strata of society. But not only does Fichte envision to turn former, essentially private and domestic education, previously limited to the few, public in form and civic in content. The state-mandated, state-regulated and state-implemented education also is to turn national and civic in the sense of including the entire population and shaping its diverse citizenry into a unitary body of civically socialized subjects.

The illiberal implications if not intentions apparent in Fichte's closed commercial and cultural state also manifest themselves in his radical program for university reform.[45] Unlike the competing and historically influential liberal proposal of Wilhelm von Humboldt, which focused on the university's requirement of freedom in research and teaching and maintained the severance of the (sought) state funding of universities from the (rejected) curricular control of higher education by the state, Fichte seeks to turn universities into higher schools for the inculcation of superior knowledge and the insinuation of a civic ethos. As in the politico-pedagogical precedent of Plato's republic, the philosophical outlook that is to inform the mode and substance of Fichte's strict system of public, profoundly political education is a highly abstract, "speculative" philosophy removed from general intelligibility but deemed without intellectual competitor or alternative and made to bear on the individual, social and civic lives of the citizens.

Fichte himself recognizes the deep affinity between his own, thoroughly abstract and theoretical philosophy, turned—or rather, conceived to become—practical and even political, and Plato's similar thinking. In particular, Fichte considers Plato a precursor of his in the focus they share on "knowledge" (*Wissen*), rather than "being" (*Sein*), as the primary object of philosophical study and effort. In Fichte's perspective on the history of philosophy, the two are united in replacing the prevalent focus of philosophy before and after Plato on being with that on knowledge.[46] Plato's theory of absolute ideas (Forms) and Fichte's theory of absolute knowledge each consider the principal grounds of all and any being to reside in knowledge, more precisely in logically and ontologically refined knowledge, devoid of the deficient features of opinion and prejudice, and considered alone to possess true being.

Their profound and pervasive communalities notwithstanding, Plato's and Fichte's political philosophy and their associated philosophical politics also exhibit considerable divergences, which are largely owed to the fundamental politico-philosophical differences between the ancient and the modern world. In particular, Fichte shares and even champions the modern moral conviction of human equality, a religiously inspired cultural legacy originating in Renaissance humanism, Protestant reformation and European Enlightenment and culminating in Kant's assigning of moral dignity—moral freedom along with moral responsibility—to each and every human being as such. By contrast, ancient thinking about matters ethical and political, including Plato's extreme emendation of it, remained marked by entrenched and ineliminable social distinctions and civic ranks. The widely shared ancient definition of human beings as capable of the exercise of reason chiefly pertained to their cognitive abilities and left the moral and civic status of human beings depend on other factors, chiefly birth and education.

Where the ancients had defined human beings largely in terms of their common reasoning faculty, the moderns—from Hobbes through Rousseau to Kant and his successors—had made the will and its self-determined exercise of choice ("freedom") the defining mark of genuinely human existence, only to submit the latter at once to rules and regulations designed to enable and ensure the possible coexistence of freely willing individuals under conditions of competition and conflict. The basic device employed by modern political philosophy for ensuring socially shared freedom was the principle of human equality—the regard and recognition of each and everyone, in the relevant group, as being of the same status and possessing the same kind and measure of freedom. The latter could be largely limited to personal freedom at the expense of political freedom, as notoriously so in Hobbes, or inclusive of political freedom, as famously so in Rousseau.

The cultural fallout of a specifically modern political philosophy and its associated philosophical politics, with their primary focus on equal freedom, has been the pervasive sociocultural and economico-political egalitarianism of modern society that emerged in the wake of the American and French Revolutions, as epitomized in the latter's political slogan "freedom, equality, brotherhood" (*liberté, égalité, fraternité*), which places the free sociality to be sought by modern philosophy and politics under a universally distributed condition of equality. In the egalitarian expectation that shapes and drives modern, "democratic" political theory and practice equality enables as much as confines freedom in the modern world. The egalitarian conception of freedom brings about the latter's ever more universal extension to each and all, but also its intentional hollowing out, to the point of creating essentially identical individuals devoid of truly distinctive marks and discriminating abilities—seemingly single individuals that exercise their freedom in altogether predictable ways.[47]

Fichte's political philosophy partakes in the modern move toward equality in matters of personal freedom and civic association. The primary category in Fichte's egalitarian program of socialized freedom is the "nation."[48] The term formerly had served to identify the geo-ethnic identity of a population comprising parts or all of an established political body. In the historical situation of medieval and early modern Europe marked by heterogeneous populations encompassed by a single political entity, or one such people stretching across established political borders, the term "nation" did not serve to identify a particular civico-political state but the population, or a part thereof, contained in a given body politic.

With the overthrow of absolutist royal rule in the French Revolution and its aftermath, the nation—first and foremost, the French nation—turned from the impotent populace of a political body to the sovereign subject of the newly constituted republic.[49] Moreover, the nation so politically constituted and empowered took it upon itself to enter the scene of international politics as an independent player in a role previously exercised by monarchical rulers and did so assisted by a popular army (*levée en masse*) in replacement of the former forcefully recruited military means.

When the heritage of the French Revolution was taken up and transformed by Napoléon Bonaparte, a former revolutionary war general turned quasi-monarchical ruler and the self-stylized emperor not "of France" but of "the French people" (*Empéreur des Français*), the term "French nation" took on the political character of an international aggressor and expansive force bent on turning dynastically diverse and politically divided Europe into a single empire subject to a reigning nation and its dominant political culture.

The nationalization of French internal and foreign politics provoked an analogous nationalization in the French-occupied parts of Europe, chiefly in Prussia, which was Fichte's adopted home country since his move from Jena to Berlin in 1799. The common political enemy served to unite not only Prussian society internally through a movement of social solidarization under conditions of foreign occupation and French governmental control. It also fostered a growing awareness of a comprehensive national identity with political significance reaching beyond the territorial borders of the many individual states that constituted as much as divided the German lands.

Fichte's politico-philosophical works from the middle of the first decade of the nineteenth century[50] partake in the widespread discovery—or rather, invention—and promotion of the novel political category of the nation. The very notion of a "German nation" (*deutsche Nation*), emphatically employed by Fichte in his *Addresses to the German Nation* from 1807–1808, was as much inspired by the model of the revolutionary French nation as it was provoked by the emerging empire of that one nation over the rest of Europe.

Accordingly, the concept of a German nation in Fichte is primarily political and not ethnic, and much less racial. Moreover, the political nature of Fichte's "German nation" is centered around the feature of freedom—of the internal freedom of the "German nation" from the absolutist rule of local princes and of the external freedom of the "German nation" from the imperialist rule of an usurpatory universal monarchy.

Moreover, the "German nation" envisioned and encouraged by Fichte is republican in character. It involves the self-constitution of a people previously divided into the populations of distinct local and regional principalities into a united body politic with a unified populace. While still ostensibly referring to monarchical rule, the new political entity to be created—or rather self-created—is to impose demands and limits on its royal ruler. The nation-state that is to emerge out of the liberation from foreign, French rule also is to involve freedom from arbitrary rule on the part of any reempowered or newly installed rulers. For the long-term future Fichte even envisions and novelistically portrays a "republic of the Germans" (*Republik der Deutschen*).[51]

Not only is the unification of the German lands advocated by Fichte politically based and civically minded, at the exclusion of ethnic distinction or racial discrimination. The identity and extent of the "German nation" is not based on geographic factors, such as natural borders, either. For Fichte the defining marks of the "German nation" are primarily cultural and ultimately political. Fichte cites as the formative feature of the people comprising the future "German nation" their long and lasting history of political independence from foreign rule, in contradistinction to the other European peoples or nations once conquered and provincialized by Rome and, on Fichte's assessment, still marked by the historical superimposition of an assimilated alien culture.[52]

Fichte casts the historical differences that continue to divide formerly Roman-occupied and historically free Europe in linguistic terms as the division between the Romance and Germanic languages spoken in modern Europe, effectively including all of Northern Europe under the designation "German nation." Moreover, he considers the binary branching of the European languages to be the manifestation of a more comprehensive, cultural differentiation into a Romance culture of regularity and refinement, on the one hand, and a Germanic culture of frugality and freedom, on the other hand. Again the difference detected by Fichte is not ethnic in character or basis but cultural and civico-political. Accordingly, Fichte allows and even envisions a future "republic of the European peoples" (*europäische Völkerrepublik*).[53] In such an international republic or republican supernation the diverse cultural nations or national cultures do not remain within the confines their particular political states but contribute actively and interactively to a larger world-historical whole. Fichte goes so far as to sever the designations "German" and "foreign" from their actual historical meanings tied to specific countries and distinct peoples—essentially the Germanic and the Romance countries—turning them instead into functional designations for the two basic kinds of persons or mind-sets to be found in the modern world, regardless of apparent national identity.[54]

More specifically, Fichte classifies modern Europe into two imaginary nations, composed of firm believers in the "dead" order of things and ardent admirers of the "living" order of freedom, respectively.[55] The duality is based on Fichte's prior twofold distinction of the types of philosophy there are, with one articulating the basic conviction of the primacy of fixed being or thinghood ("dogmatism") and the other taking free being-for-itself or selfhood ("idealism") as the basis and core of a given human being's entire thinking and doing.[56] By politicizing and, as it were, nationalizing the meta-philosophical distinction between thing-thinkers and freedom-thinkers, Fichte turns the contingent historical opposition between the Romance world and the Germanic world in general and between France and Germany in particular, into a functional differentiation of two systematic types and historical shapes of human cultural existence.

The political point behind the sociocultural dualism in European history as diagnosed by Fichte is not the consolidation of Europe's division along established or newly emerging national lines and in terms of nationalist mentalities. Rather, Fichte envisions the political developments at the national level, in particular the effective republicanization of a future German state borne by the civic self-unification of the "German nation," to prepare the way for a "common nation" (*gemeinsame Nation*).[57] On Fichte's account, nationalism and its political ally—civic patriotism—represent a suitable step and a mandated means in an overall international world-historical process that stretches from the ancient to the modern world and from the past through to the present, and that aims at turning nationals of particular states into citizens of a shared political world order of federal constitution and republican character in the tradition of Kant's contractual script for political history, *Toward Perpetual Peace*.[58]

But the limitations that Fichte places on European and especially German nationalism are not exhausted by the future prospect and purpose of an international political federation and its associated world citizenship. Even at the level of the actual nation state, the civic identity of the subject, on Fichte's assessment, precedes and exceeds the confines of a given national community. Fichte's political philosophy of freedom conjoins the merely instrumental function that the individual nation possesses for the preparation of an international order with the essentially subservient role of the state for establishing and ensuring the personal and civic freedom of its citizen subjects. Fichte regards neither the state qua political society nor the nation as the state's popular justificatory basis as an end in itself.

As Kant before him, Fichte reserves the status of an end in itself to the human individual as such, defined as a freely willing being under self-imposed rational laws (autonomy). For Fichte political law and order at the national and international level is to be mindful of the subjects' original, prepolitical freedom and to have its juridico-political measures geared at the cultivation of that freedom ("culture for freedom"; *Kultur zur Freiheit*)[59]—a cultivation that the state is to enable and enhance but which only the individual as such can undertake and achieve. The focus on the freedom that human beings possess prior to their specifically political association and that they are to continue to enjoy within the state permeates Fichte's political philosophy even as it turns national under contemporary circumstances and removes him, again, from too close a similarity with Plato.

State and Realm

Fichte's continuing commitment to the preservation and cultivation of the distinct, self-determined existence of the originally free human being, independent of the prevailing political strictures of the state and the constraining civic conditioning of the nation finds its final formulation in his late political philosophy of history. Originally announced as "lectures of varied content" on matters of "applied politics," the work was published posthumously under the title "The Doctrine of the State" (*Die Staatslehre*).[60] Fichte's last larger work combines a weighty introductory part on the systematic place of politics in philosophy in general and in the philosophy of right in particular with an outline of the juridico-political course of human history from inequality and unfreedom to equal freedom and from the political privileging of law and right to their equal distribution and universal extension.[61]

Fichte's late treatment of the state aims at the integration of political philosophy, philosophy of right and philosophy of history into a unified, historically informed and systematically structured account of the idea of right. For Fichte human history is essentially the history of the successive theoretical and practical realization of the concept of right as the primary feature of free intelligent beings. In essence, right for Fichte is the right to be and to remain free. As in Kant's and in Fichte's own earlier political thought, right concerns the external freedom of actions in the exercise of choice under the guidance of reason. Given the plurality of individual human beings engaged in the practice of freely chosen action, right takes on the function of establishing and ensuring the possible coexistence of externally free acting in a shared social sphere.

Again in continuity with Kant's and his own earlier views on the matter, the later Fichte accords the task of guaranteeing the socially compatible exercise of right to the political institution of the state. The latter is to be respectful of original, prepolitical, "natural" law and right and charged with the latter's assurance by means of positive right and law. To that effect, the political state is exclusively endowed with the entitlement ("right") to constrain any use of external freedom actually or potentially injurious to everyone's equal right to freedom.

But Fichte's late "political science" does not leave it at the presentation of a doctrinal body of juridico-political principles that may find themselves unrealized and not respected in most, if not all of actual human history. In addition to setting forth the norms that are to regulate politics and its institutional implementation of right,

Fichte seeks to map his essentially juristic conception of politics onto the course of human history in its past, present and future unfolding. In particular, he seeks to uncover the laws and structures underlying the apparent plurality and diversity of historical developments. The regularity so detected in human history is to provide an indication of the overall course and the eventual endpoint of human existence in history understood in terms of the political development of right.

Kant's similarly oriented attempt at a juristically focused human history "with a cosmopolitan intent" still had resorted to teleological vocabulary and conceptuality, maintaining purpose, design or intention on the part of "Nature," even as he sought to reduce the traditional teleological discourse to the status of a hypothesis or fiction ("as if"). By contrast, Fichte ventures a nonteleological, outright mechanical, if not mechanistic account of the forces that underlie human history, which, however, are not considered sufficient to completely determine the course of history. Moreover, the competing forces so introduced, distinguished and interrelated at the basis of actual history are not located in some agency or nature outside and independent of the human beings. Rather, Fichte considers the principal factors shaping history to form an integral part of the human beings themselves—more precisely, of their essence or nature as freely willing intelligent agents.

Most importantly, in Fichte's late political philosophy the historically effective forces and factors that form part of human rational nature do not operate blindly and mechanically, as though driven by physical necessity, but are the object of a rationally motivated and essentially free employment brought about by human willing and acting. For the late Fichte, human history as the history of political right not only concerns and involves human beings but follows and serves them, being the result of prior human choices as much as setting the stage for further such choices.

According to the late Fichte, there are two principles underlying human political history inherent in human rational nature as such, those of order and freedom, with the former ensuring the unity and communal character of human actions and the latter representing the requirement of self-determined willing and acting. In psychological terms, Fichte associates the fundamental human allegiance to social order with the attitude of "faith" (*Glaube*), stressing the element of unquestioned, "blind" conviction based on a recognized authority in matters of the regulation of conduct. By contrast, he correlates the basic human affinity to freedom with the cognitive requirement of "understanding" (*Verstand*), stressing the intellectual prerequisite of having obedience, compliance or any other kind of conformity in conduct based on one's own "insight" (*Einsicht*).[62]

At the historical level, Fichte locates the two principles of human agency in two alterative original populations or "peoples" that he imagines to have constituted the two, equally essential elements of effective historical developmental change. The first of the two societies is portrayed as living in blind obedience to laws disclosed in a prepolitical process removed from scrutiny and investigation, termed "revelation" (*Offenbarung*).[63] As long as this first people remains by itself, its society, according to Fichte, will remain in a stable condition maintained by obediently followed customary laws governing family life and wider social life forms. A primitive society of this type may enjoy peace and even approach the state of an earthly paradise in which life lacks the formal framework of enforced right and constrained freedom that is definitive of political society or the state. Accordingly, a stateless original society of this type also lacks substantial change and for that matter any real history. The second type of original society introduced by Fichte's speculations on the "conjectural beginning of human history" (Kant) is marked by a wild freedom not ruled by principles. A human society of this form is involved in constant change without being able to successfully settle on a direction and a goal for its endless pursuits.

Fichte's imaginary scenario of originary humanity prior to its historico-political development as being divided into an obediently ordered and a wildly free kind of people, recalls the biblical narrative about the primeval social antagonism between Cain and Abel or between city dwellers and nomads. On Fichte's account, though, neither of the two social life forms is dispensable for the first beginning and the further development of human history. Moreover, according to Fichte, only the joining of order and freedom and the concomitant proper interpenetration of faith and understanding can initiate and ensure humanity's entry into history, which is a history of human making and one oriented toward humanity's own, self-given and self-made end at that.[64]

As Fichte details further, for human history to begin at all and to continue to unfold it is not sufficient that two such peoples meet and merge. As long as one of the two opposed proto-peoples involved prevails over the other one, the newly created aggregate will revert to the condition of the victor. On Fichte's account, humanity's entrance into history requires quite specifically that the second, wildly free people, while retaining the basic sense of their freedom, submit to the very idea of a social life governed by rules as represented, however inadequately, in the blind obedience of the law-abiding kind of proto-people. Only then can history in general and political history in particular unfold through the mutual infringement as well as enhancement of the two popular principles, with the first one contributing the element of lawfulness and the second one contributing to the requirement of freedom from foreign rule and extraneous regulation.

On Fichte's understanding, the historical development set into motion and continuously maintained by the interferential relations between the two people principles and their correlated principal peoples is an extended process of enlightenment in which the previously prevailing blind faith in rules and regulations of all kinds, including political laws, is gradually replaced by insight into the function and utility of social and civic regulations, which in turn informs the further refinement or revision of such rules guided by the ever increasing insight into the functional interdependence and ideal identity of freedom and right.

So strong is Fichte's conviction of the progressive juridico-political enlightenment on a global scale that he predicts the eventual falling away of the state as an instrument of constraint to be replaced with the unconstrained community of free beings who respect each other's external freedom on the basis of insight rather than out of fear of punishment or hope of reward. But Fichte is also enough of a political realist to date the transition from the political world of forceful constraint to the metapolitical world of free compliance to a remote future, the arrival of which he considers entirely contingent upon sufficient human cognitive and conative self-improvement and not guaranteed by any wisdom or cunning operative and effective behind people's backs in the manner of Kant's or Hegel's teleology of human history.

Fichte portrays the final state possibly reached in human history by human efforts alone as the "realm of law and right" (*Reich des Rechts*), the "realm of freedom" (*Reich der Freiheit*), or, in short, the "realm" (*Reich*).[65] The metapolitical realm that is to supersede the state does not so much constitute the object of a political eschatology, to be achieved at the end of historical time, but represents the free sociality that unites free beings even prior to its outwardly manifest political realization. In the counterfactual sense of Fichte's "realm," free human beings as such originally and continuously constitute an ideal community that is universal in extension and that can be considered to exist alongside the state and its multiple manifestations as individual states located in geo-space and stretching across historical time.

The (meta-)political category of the realm featured in Fichte's late political philosophy of history is informed by Judeo-Christian thinking about the reign of God, a para-political entity distinct from, opposed to and supraordinated to secular rule. But the notion of a realm also recalls and revises the transposition of this politico-theological conception into modern moral philosophy through Kant's conception of the "realm of ends" (*Reich der Zwecke*), understood as the ideal community of human beings considered as "ends in themselves," distinct from any other association in which they use each other to serve their own particular purposes.

These affinities notwithstanding, Fichte's realm is neither a divine kingdom under the lawful command of a personal God nor an ethical community under the moral law conceived, as it is in Kant, on the model of an "ethical commonwealth" (*ethisches Gemeinwesen*) or a "church" (*Kirche*).[66] Rather Fichte's realm of the free remains a body politic in the specific sense of a global civic order regulating external actions under conditions and for the purpose of communal freedom based on self-imposed and self-enacted external, juridical laws. For Fichte politics, whether it is the politics of the state's order or that of the elusive realm, remains distinct from morals, just as the normative dimension of politics—the legal sphere—remains distinct from the ethical sphere.

Prior to actually achieving the remote end of the known political world of external constraint, of legal compulsion and of juridical curtailment through the eventual installation of the free reign ("realm") of law and right, human history, for Fichte, stays tied to the political order of the state. In order to enable and facilitate the gradual world-historical transformation of the state into the realm,

Fichte has the state's system of legal constraint be embedded in civic instruction on the function and purpose of the law—a civic education centered around the justification of the law's constraining force as a necessary condition for the possibility of everyone's external freedom.

More specifically, on the later Fichte's juridico-political conception of the state, the very political body—be it a natural person or a body of persons—that possesses the power and force to exercise effective legal constraint, the "enforcer of right" (*Zwingherr zum Recht*), also serves as a civic teacher and political educator (*Erzieher, Lehrer*) aiming at enhancing and advancing popular compliance with juridical law by means of enlarged insight in its purpose and understanding of its function.[67] Accordingly, Fichte considers the office of political leadership best to be carried out by teachers and educators, due to their insight into the justificatory basis of law and right and their skill in conveying the lessons of political law to the larger populace.

While the joining of legal constraint to legal instruction in Fichte's late political science is reminiscent of the explanations that are to preface the laws in Plato's late work in political philosophy, *The Laws*,[68] the fusion of the political educator and the political ruler recalls Plato's vision of a personal union of the philosopher and the ruler in the *Republic*.[69] Fichte is clearly aware of the similarities, which extend to the overall politicization of life in the state on the latter's way to the realm. At the same time he is quite critical of contemporary attempts to invoke the political order of the ancient world, in particular that of the Greek *polis*, for modern political theory and practice, chastising the aesthetic infatuation with and the "artificial aping of the state of antiquity."[70]

Instead, Fichte insists on the juridico-political divide that separates the ancient world, including "free" Greece, from the modern world and its specifically different freedom—a freedom that is, at least in theory and increasingly so in practice, not marred by privilege and exclusion but marked by the granting and guaranteeing of freedom, notably of personal and civic freedom, to an ever wider populace. More specifically, Fichte considers it the exclusive juridico-political achievement of the modern world to have comprehended and implemented the "equality of right" (*Gleichheit des Rechts*)—a political order ruled by just laws—and to increasingly achieve the "equality of rights" (*Gleichheit der Rechte*)—of ever more equally and universally distributed legal entitlements along with their implied obligations.

Still, the republic envisioned by the late Fichte under the twin shape of the historical, quintessentially modern "state of right" and the transhistorical, essentially counterfactual "realm of freedom" is not a republic of the modern democratic kind first discovered, explored and assessed by Tocqueville on the American continent some fifteen years after Fichte's late "Political Science." The citizens of Fichte's actual state as well as the citizens of his elusive realm may enjoy personal and civic freedom in leading self-determined lives shaped by private preferences as much as by public obligations. But they lack political freedom in the sense of determining for themselves, individually and collectively, the governance of the state by the giving of laws, by enacting them and by adjudicating their observance—all tasks once upon a time and for a short time, exercised, directly if discriminately, by the fully entitled citizens of the Athenian democratic *polis*.

The manifestly antidemocratic republicanism of Fichte—a profound distrust of popular rule shared by most of his contemporaries, including Kant and Hegel—which places legislative, executive and jurisdictional powers into the hands of dedicated pedagogical and political experts informed by alleged superior intellectual insight, if not exceeding moral qualification, proved a lasting legacy of Plato's *Republic* across the great divide between ancient and modern political philosophy.

For the longest time, democratism as epitomized in ancient Athens and republicanism as exemplified by classical Rome formed distinct political legacies that have merged only fairly recently with the creation of democratic republics in the wake of the bourgeois revolutions in North America and Europe.

Democratic rule and republican governance remain in tension today. While the ancient, direct and comprehensive type of democracy may be deemed unnecessary and even inimical to a republican polity, the modern, indirect and massive form of democracy does not seem sufficient for maintaining a republican polity with its requirements of civic ethos, public responsibility and participatory politics. In light of Plato's precedent and its aftermath in classical German political philosophy, the democratic transformation of republican governance effectuated in the interest of equality calls for a reverse republican reinvigoration of popular rule in the spirit of freely active self-rule.

Appendix

"Plato Republic" (ca. 1807) by Fichte

The following text by Fichte, titled "Plato Republic" (*Platon Republik*), which had never been published, first appeared in Zöller (2011a, 209f.). The text has since been included in the final volume of the *Collected Works of J. G. Fichte* (Fichte 1962, II/17:387f.). Both publications of the text were edited by Erich Fuchs, who dates the text to the first half of 1807. It consists of a series of short notes reflecting Fichte's study of the first three books of Plato's *Republic* undertaken in the context of his own contemporary work in political philosophy. The first publication of the text was accompanied by a compilation of fifteen short passages from Fichte's published and posthumous works that refer to Plato, including references to Plato's political philosophy (Zöller 2011a).

In the following transcription of the original German text, Fichte's inadvertent orthographic mistakes have been corrected and his abbreviations for proper names have been replaced with the full names. The English translation subsequently supplied is by Günter Zöller.

Platon Republik (ca. 1807)

J. G. Fichte

Grundbegriff: der der Gerechtigkeit. Ich will diesem eben ruhig nachgehen, ob es zur Spitze kommt.

—. Jedem das gebührende zu geben.[1] Daß er nun sogleich nach *Künsten* fragt, u. die Gerechtigkeit als eine besondere Kunst, deren Objekt nicht recht ausgemittelt werden könne, sezt, macht da Verwirrungen. Z. B. ironisch: sie sey zum aufbehalten des Geldes, die Sichel: der Weinbau zum Gebrauch der Sichel.[2]

Später hin; eine Kunst des Stehlens, zum Nutzen der Freunde, u. Schaden der Feinde.[3] / Doch ist dies sonderbar herum gedreht.

In der Unterredung mit Thrasymachus läßt Socrates sich viel zu leicht alles zurechnen. Z. B. Die Gerechtigkeit sey die Tugend der Seele![4] Wie konnte Thrasymachus dies zugeben.

Zu Ende des Buchs wird jedoch treflich eingelenkt.

2tes Buch

Man wolle die Gerechtigkeit zuförderst in *gröberer* Schrift, am Staate, kennen lernen.—.[5] Ueber die *Lüge*: Dieselbe dem Regenten allenfals erlaubt, aber dem Bürger, als gegen das *allgemeine Intereße* laufend, verboten.[6] / Sehr bedeutend, und stimmt mit meinen Grundsätzen über den Kontrakt überein.

3tes Buch

Man müsse, wie von Göttern und Helden nicht schlecht, also auch von Menschen nicht sagen, daß der Gerechte unglüklich, der Ungerechte aber glüklich lebe.[7] (So wie die beiden Brüder zu anfange des 2ten Buchs geredet hatten.[8]). Geben Sie nun dies zu, so hätten sie alles frühere zugegeben, und ihre eigne Rede zurükgenommen. Sonderbarer, u. täuschender Uebergang.

"Plato Republic" (ca. 1807)

J. G. Fichte

Basic concept: that of justice. I will simply follow the latter [and see] whether there is a pinnacle [to the argument].[9]

—. To give everyone what is owed to him.[10] That he now immediately inquires into the *arts*, and posits justice as a special art, the object of which reportedly cannot be properly ascertained, causes confusions there. E.g., ironically: it [i.e. justice] is supposedly there for the safekeeping of money, the sickle: [that] viniculture [exists] for the use of the sickle.[11] Later on: an art of stealing, to the advantage of friends, and the hurt of enemies.[12] / Yet this is strangely twisted.

In the dialogue with Thrasymachus Socrates far too easily gets everything conceded to himself. E.g., [that] justice is the virtue of the soul![13] How could Thrasymachus concede that. Toward the end of the Book, however, there is some fine relenting.

2nd Book

That one wants to get to know justice first in *coarser* writing, in the state.—.[14] On the *lie*: That the latter at most is permitted to the regent, but prohibited to the citizen, as running contrary to the *general interest.*[15] / Very significant, and agrees with my principles on the contract.

3rd Book

That just as one is not to speak badly of gods and heroes, so one is not to say of human beings that the just one lives unhappy, but the unjust one lives happy.[16] (As the two brothers had spoken at the beginning of Book 2.[17]). If they were to concede this, they would have conceded everything [said] earlier, and would have taken back their own speech. Strange and deceptive transition.

Notes

Chapter 1 The Polity: Plato and the Republican Legacy

1 Kant 1900, 19:566 (*Reflexion* 7964).

2 See Popper 1945.

3 For an account of the Western republican tradition from antiquity to the American Revolution, see Rahe 1992.

4 On a certain Greek ancestry of republicanism, see Nelson 2004.

5 See *Politics* 3.7 (1279a22–1279b10); Aristotle 1985, 2:2030. See also *Statesman* 302c–d; Plato 1985, 1073.

6 On the tradition of the mixed constitution in Plato, Aristotle and Polybius, see Hahm 2009.

7 For a succinct account of Roman republican institutions in their politico-historical context, see Gwynn 2012, esp. 18–24.

8 See Pocock 2010, 146f.

9 See *Politics* 4.2 and 4.8 (1289a26–39 and 1293b23–1294a8); Aristotle 1985, 2:2046 and 2053f.

10 See Nelson 2010.

11 On early modern "civic republicanism," see Baron 1955 and Pocock 1975. On the kind of freedom involved in classical republicanism, see Skinner 2012.

12 On the limited contribution of the third chief representative of German idealism, Schelling, to classical German political philosophy, see Zöller 2014d.

13 For a recent revival of republicanism in an essentially liberal Anglo-American context, focusing on freedom as non-domination, see Pettit 1997.

Chapter 2 The Ideal Republic: Kant and Plato

1 Hume 1987, 94 ("Of Civil Liberty") (in the original emphasis).

2 For a cultural history of republican governance, see Everdell 2000.

3 On Kant's acquaintance with ancient philosophy and its significance for his philosophical development, see Reich 1935 and Santozki 2006.

4 See Kant 1900, 4:255 (*Prolegomena to Any Future Metaphysics*); Kant 2002, 53.

5 See Kant 1781/1787, A VII-XII, A 856/B 884.

6 See Kant 1900, 8:341–386 and 8:411–422; Kant 1996b, 317–351. See Zöller 2003c.

7 See Kant 1781/1787, A 852/B 880–A 856/B 884.

8 Kant 1781/1787, A 853/B 881.

9 See Kant 1781/1787, A 852/B 880–A 856/B 884.

10 See, e.g., Kant 1900, 17:556 (Refl. 4450; "mystical principles" in Plato), 17:686 (*Reflexion* 4718; Plato a "mystical idealist"), 18:15 (*Reflexion* 4868; "mystical *intellectualia*" in Plato) and 18:21 (*Reflexion* 4893; "mystical origin of noumuena" in Plato); only the last reference is included in Kant 2005 (198).

11 Kant 8:387–406; Kant 2002, 429–445.

12 On Kant's distinction between theoretical and practical philosophy, his identification of practical philosophy with moral philosophy and his distinction between (juridical) law and ethics, see Kant 1900, 5:171–173 (*Critique of the Power of Judgment*), 20:195–206 (*First Introduction to the Critique of the Power of Judgment*) and 6:214–221 (*The Metaphysics of Morals*); Kant 2000, 59–61, Kant 2000, 3–11 and Kant 1996b, 370–376.

13 Kant 1781/1787, A 310/B 366–A 338/B 396.

14 See Kant 1781/1787, A 312/B 368–A 320/B 377.

15 On the status and role of ideas in Kant's theory of reason, Zöller 2011c and 2013a.

16 See Kant 1781/1787, A 81/B 107.

17 See Kant 1781/1787, A 312–314/B 368–371.

18 See also Kant's classification of ideas qua representations in Kant 1781/1787, A 320/376f. On the modern "way of ideas," see Cummins and Zöller 1993.

19 In view of the terminological and conceptual continuity between *ideai* and *eide* in Plato and *Ideen* in Kant, the customary English designation,

"Forms," for Plato's idea-objects will be replaced from here on by the term "ideas," used in an objective, nonmental sense.

20 This is Kant's own image. See Kant 1781/1787, A 314/B 370f.

21 Kant 1781/1787, A 313/B 370 (translation modified).

22 Kant 1781/1787, A 313/B 370 (translation modified).

23 Kant 1781/1787, A 313/B 370.

24 See Kant 1781/1787, A 313/B 370.

25 See Kant 1781/1787, A 314/B 370. A sustained exercise in such a reading of Plato is the comprehensive Plato interpretation of the leading neo-Kantian philosopher Paul Natorp. See Natorp 1903.

26 Kant 1781/1787, A 314 note/B 371 note (translation modified).

27 Kant 1781/1787, A 315/B 371.

28 Kant 1781/1787, A 165/B 206.

29 Kant 1781/1787, A 315/B 371f (translation modified).

30 Kant 1781/1787, A 318/B 375 (translation modified).

31 Kant 1781/1787, A 317/B 374.

32 Kant 1781/1787, A 318/B 375 (translation modified).

33 Kant 1781/1787, A 319/B 375 (translation modified).

34 Kant 1781/1787, A 318/B 375.

35 Kant 1781/1787, A 316/B 372 (in the original emphasis).

36 Kant 1781/1787, A 316/B 372 (translation modified).

37 Kant 1781/1787, A 316/B 373.

38 Kant 1781/1787, A 316/B 373 (translation modified).

39 Kant 1781/1787, A 316/B 373.

40 Kant 1781/1787, A 317/B 374.

41 Kant 1781/1787, A 316/B 373 (in the original emphasis) (translation modified).

42 See Kant 1990, 8:15–31 (*Idea for a Universal History with a Cosmopolitan Aim*); Kant 2007, 108–120.

43 See Kant 1990, 8:289–306; Kant 1996b, 290–304.

44 See Kant 1990, 8:341–386; Kant 1996b, 317–351.

45 See Kant 1990, 7:77–94; Kant 1996a, 295–309.

46 See Kant 1990, 6:229–372; Kant 1996b, 386–506.

47 On the development of Kant's cultural-political thought, see Zöller 2014b.

48 See Kant 1990, 6:313 (*The Metaphysics of Morals*); Kant 1996b, 456f.

49 Kant 1990, 6:311 and 318 (*The Metaphysics of Morals*); Kant 1996b, 455 and 461.
50 See Kant 1990, 8:290–296; Kant 1996b, 290–296.
51 See Kant 1990, 8:349–352 (*Toward Perpetual Peace*); Kant 1996b, 322–324.
52 Kant 1990, 6:340 (*The Metaphysics of Morals*); Kant 1996b, 480.
53 Kant 1990, 6:340 (*The Metaphysics of Morals*); Kant 1996b, 480 (translation modified).
54 See Kant 1900, 6:338 (*The Metaphysics of Morals*); Kant 1996b, 479.
55 See Kant 1990, 6:329, 6:313–315 and 8:352 (*The Metaphysics of Morals, Toward Perpetual Peace*); Kant 1996b, 470f., 456–459 and 324.
56 See Kant 1990, 7:91 (*The Conflict of the Faculties*); Kant 1996a, 306 (translation modified).
57 See Kant 1990, 6:321f. (*The Metaphysics of Morals*); Kant 1996b, 465.
58 See Kant 1990, 8:36–38 (*An Answer to the Question: What Is Enlightenment?*); Kant 1991, 55f. On the political requirement of publicity, see Kant 1990, 8:381 (*Perpetual Peace*); Kant 1996b, 347.
59 See Kant 1990, 6:341 (*The Metaphysics of Morals*); Kant 1996b, 481 (translation modified). See also Kant 1990, 8:352f. (*Perpetual Peace*); Kant 1996b, 324f.
60 For an idealized portrayal of the Athenian democratic *ethos*, see Pericles's funeral oration for the war dead at the end of the first year of the Peloponnesian War in Thucydides 1996, 111–118, esp. 113f. (bk. 2, chap. 40).
61 See Kant 1900, 6:307f. (*The Metaphysics of Morals*); Kant 1996b, 451f.
62 See Kant 1900, 8:26 (*Idea For a Universal History with a Cosmopolitan Aim*); Kant 2007, 116. On Kant's political philosophy of history and political anthropology, see Zöller 2011b and 2014a.

Chapter 3 The Real Republic: Hegel and Plato

1 Guillois 1889, 2:395. The epigraph is Napoleon Bonaparte to Johann Wolfgang Goethe during their personal meeting in Erfurt in October 1808. The phrase was recorded by the latter in German as *Die Politik ist jetzt das Schicksal* (Goethe 1994, 381) and had to be retranslated into French. With the phrase Napoleon was replying somewhat dismissively to Goethe's reference to the role of fate in ancient tragic thinking,

arguing that in modern times the role of fate (or destiny) had been taken over by politics.

2 See, e.g., Marx 1970 and Popper 1945.

3 For Hegel's philosophy of the history of philosophy, see Hegel 1983, vol. 6; Hegel 1968, vol. 1.

4 Hegel 1983, 8:50; Hegel 1968, 90 (translation modified). Hegel employs the German word *Republic* rather than the term *Staat* ("state") to refer to Plato's *Politeia.*

5 See Hegel 1983, 8:6f.; Hegel 1968, 12f.

6 Hegel 1983, 8:7; Hegel 1968, 13.

7 See Hegel 1989, vols. 19 and 20.

8 See Hegel 1989, 8:1–21; Hegel 1968, 1–49.

9 See Hegel 1989, 8:21–36; Hegel 1968, 49–71.

10 See Hegel 1989, 8:37–49; Hegel 1968, 71–90.

11 See Hegel 1989, 8:49–58; Hegel 1968, 90–117.

12 See Kant 1781/1787, B 274.

13 See Kant 1781/1787, A 367–380.

14 See Kant 1781/1787, B 274–277.

15 See Kant 1781/1787, A 26/B 42–A 30/B 45 and A 32/B 49–A 36/B 53.

16 A 28/B 44 and A 36/B 52. See also Kant 1900, 18:646 (Refl. 6324).

17 See Kant's "division of the concept of nothing" in Kant 1781/1787, A 292/B 348.

18 See Fichte 1962, III/3:224–281, esp. 245; Jacobi 1994, 497–536, esp. 519.

19 See Hegel 1989, 12:173–253; Hegel 2010, 670–753.

20 "See the section "From Categories to Ideas" in Chapter 1 above.

21 See Kant 1781/1787, A 642/B 670–A 668/B 696.

22 See Kant 1900, 122–134; Kant 1996b, 238–247.

23 See Hegel 1989, 9:53–62; Hegel 1977, 46–57.

24 See Hegel 1989, 19:287–416 and 20:379–572; partial translation in Hegel 1978.

25 See Hegel 1989, 14,1:278–282; Hegel 1991, 377–380.

26 Hegel 1989, 12:355, 366; Hegel 2011, 399, 406.

27 Hegel 1989, 12:380; Hegel 2011, 416.

28 See Hegel 1989, 12:357; Hegel 2011, 400.

29 See Hegel 1989, 12:363, 372; Hegel 2011, 404, 410 and 363.

30 Hegel 1989, 12:358; Hegel 2011, 401.

31 See Hegel 1989, 12:379f.; Hegel 2011, 415f.
32 See Hegel 1989, 12:381f.; Hegel 2011, 417f.
33 See Hegel 1989, 12: 361f.; Hegel 2011, 402.
34 Hegel 1989, 12:380f.; Hegel 2011, 416f.
35 Hegel 1989, 12:360; Hegel 2011, 402.
36 Hegel 1983, 8:50f.; Hegel 1968, 98f.
37 Hegel 1989, 14,1:14; Hegel 1991, 20.
38 See section "From Plato's Ideas to Kant's Ideas" in Chapter 2 above.
39 See Hegel 1983, 8:9–12; Hegel 1968, 22–242.
40 Hegel 1983, 8:51; Hegel 1968, 96 (translation modified).
41 See Hegel 1983, 8:51; Hegel 1968, 96.
42 See Hegel 1989, 12:372f.; Hegel 2011, 410f.
43 See Hegel 1983, 8:58; Hegel 1968, 114f.
44 See Hegel 1989, 14,1; Hegel 1991. For Hegel's relation to the tradition of natural law, see Hegel 1989, 4:417–485; Hegel 1975a. On the early development of Hegel's political philosophy in context of southwest German Protestantism and Scottish Enlightenment, see Dickey 1987.
45 On the liberating function of juridical laws in Hegel, see Conklin 2008. For a general account of Hegel as a political philosopher of the modern state, see Taylor 1979.
46 On the organological imagery of the members of body politic, see Zöller 2014a.
47 See Hegel 1989, 14,1:51–97; Hegel 1991, 66–132.
48 See Hegel 1989, 14,1:99–136; Hegel 1991, 133–186.
49 See Hegel 1989, 14,1:137–355; Hegel 1991, 187–380. On the embeddedness of Hegel's political philosophy of the state in his political philosophy of society, see Avineri 1972.
50 See Hegel 1989, 14,1:144–159; Hegel 1991, 199–219.
51 See Hegel 1989, 14,1:160–200; Hegel 1991, 220–274.
52 See Hegel 1989, 14,1:201–282; Hegel 1991, 275–380.
53 Hegel 1989, 14,1:226; Hegel 1991, 308.
54 See Hegel 1989, 14,1:232; Hegel 1991, 317.
55 See Hegel 1989, 14,1:211f.; Hegel 1991, 288. For a republican reading of Hegel in the tradition of "civic humanism," see Patten 1999, esp. 166–201.
56 See Hegel 1983, 8:57f.; Hegel 1968, 109–112.
57 See Hegel 1989, 12:362f. and 383; Hegel 2011, 404 and 418.

58 See Hegel 1989, 14,1:249f. and 254f.; Hegel 1991, 339f. and 347f.
59 *Laws* 739a3; Plato 1985, 1324.

Chapter 4 The People's Republic: Fichte and Plato

1 *Nicomachean Ethics* 1253a31f.; Aristotle 1985, 2:1988, alternatively Aristotle 1998, 11.
2 On the presence of Fichte in Plato's work, see Wundt 1929.
3 On Fichte's philosophical project of a transcendental philosophy of mind and world, see Zöller 1998.
4 Kant 1781/1787, B 112–116.
5 Kant 1781/1787, B 160 note and A 292/B 348.
6 Kant 1781/1787, B 305.
7 See Fichte 1962, I/2:255–264; Fichte 1982, 93–102.
8 See Fichte 1962, I/4:276; Fichte 1994, 113f.
9 See Fichte 1962, II/10:30f.
10 See Fichte 1962, II/6:143–206.
11 See Fichte 1962, II/8:33, 131, 241; Fichte WL 1804/II 23, 43, 89.
12 On the overall development and continuous unity of Fichte's philosophy, see Zöller 2013b.
13 See Fichte 1962, I/2:48, 57 and 65; Fichte 1988, 65, 70, 75 and Fichte 1962, I/4:278; Fichte 1994, 115.
14 See Fichte 1962, I/2:255; Fichte 1982, 93.
15 See Kant 1781/1787, B 116.
16 See Fichte 1962, I/2:112–118; Fichte 1988, 101–106.
17 For the term "noumenalism," see Zöller 1998, 111–116.
18 See section "From Plato's Ideas to Kant's Ideas" in Chapter 2 above.
19 See Kant 1781/1787, A 820/B 848–A 831/B 859 and Kant 1900, 5:142–146; Kant 1996b, 254–257.
20 Fichte 1962, I/2:397; Fichte 1982, 231.
21 Fichte 1962, I/2:431, Fichte 1982, 266.
22 For Fichte's popular philosophical project on the vocation of the human being in general and that of the scholar in particular, see Fichte 1962, I/6:189–309, I/3:23–68, I/6:183–311 and II/12:313–363; Fichte 1999, 1:319–478, 1:47–205 and 207–317.
23 See Fichte 1962, II/8:24.
24 See Fichte 1962, I/10:148; Fichte 1968, 51. For the explicit identification

of *Gesicht* qua *visum* and "idea" qua Form, see Fichte 1962, II/12:315. See also Fichte 1962, II/12:173. For Fichte's rare use of the plural, *Gesichte*, meaning "visions," see Fichte 1962, II/12:326.

25 On the status and function of visual metaphors in Fichte, see Zöller 2014e.

26 See Fichte 1962, II/10:166f. and 171.

27 See Fichte 1962, I/2:365; Fichte 1982, 198f.

28 See Fichte 1962, I/7:249.

29 Fichte 1962, 338.

30 See *Republic* 508b–e and 516b; Plato 1985, 743f. and 748f.

31 On the overall political character of Fichte's philosophy, see Zöller 2014c.

32 See *Republic* 368c–369 a; Plato 1985, 615.

33 See *Republic* 435b–c; Plato 1985, 677.

34 See section "The Prehistory of the History of Philosophy" in Chapter 2 above.

35 See section "Kant's Republicanism" in Chapter 2 above.

36 Fichte 1962, I/3:417f.; Fichte 2000, 117. See also Fichte 1962, I/3:412f.; Fichte 2000, 111f. See section "Kant's Republicanism" in Chapter 2 above.

37 See Fichte 1962, I/3:434f.; Fichte 2000, 135f.

38 See Zöller 2011a.

39 See section "Kant's Republicanism" in Chapter 2 above.

40 GA I/4:17; Fichte 2000, 179.

41 See GA I/1:204.

42 See the appendix: "Plato Republic" (ca. 1807) by Fichte. See also GA II/17:387f.

43 See Fichte 1962, I/7:37–141; Fichte 2012.

44 See Fichte 1962, I/10:117–142 and 213–284; Fichte 1968, 16–44 and 130–210.

45 See Fichte 1962, II/11:83–170.

46 See GA II/9:181.

47 This is also Tocqueville's critical analysis of modern representative mass democracy in Tocqueville 2000. On the affinities between classical German political philosophy and Tocqueville's sociopolitical science, see Zöller 2014a.

48 See Fichte 1962, I/10:110 and 179, Fichte 1968, 8 and 88.

49 For the contemporary coinage of the term, see Sieyès 2003.
50 See Fichte 1962, I/9:393–445; Fichte 1962, I/10:97–298; Fichte 1968; Fichte 1962, II/10:377–426. See also Fichte 1962, I/8:189–396; Fichte 1999, 2:VII–X and 1–288.
51 See Fichte 1962, II/10:377–426.
52 See Fichte 1962, I/10:143–170; Fichte 1968, 45–77.
53 Fichte 1971, 7:572.
54 See Fichte 1962, I/4:14; Fichte 2000, 176. For an internationalist reading of Fichte's *Addresses to the German Nation*, see Zöller 2008.
55 See Fichte 1962, I/10:183–197; Fichte 1968, 92–110.
56 See Fichte 1962, I/4:118 and 195 (SW I, 426 and 434). See also Fichte 1962, I/10:184; Fichte 1968, 93.
57 Fichte 1962, I/10:168; Fichte 1968, 75 (translation modified).
58 On the ultimate identity of patriotism and cosmopolitanism, see Fichte 1962, I/9:399. On the civic rather than nationalist character of patriotism, see Fichte 1962, I/10:198–212; Fichte 1968, 111–129.
59 On Fichte's civico-political understanding of culture, see Fichte 1962, I/1:244. For the civico-pedagogical project titled "culture for freedom," see Fichte 1962, I/1:249.
60 See Fichte 1962, II/16:13–204. For further material on Fichte's late theologico-political project, see GA II/15:203–404.
61 For a more detailed account of Fichte's *Doctrine of the State* that focuses on the work's political philosophy of law, education and religion, see Zöller 2009 and Zöller 2011d.
62 See Fichte 1962, II/16:109f.
63 Fichte 1962, II/16:103.
64 See Fichte 1962, II/16:110.
65 Fichte 1962, II/16:53, 131 and 164. See also the realm's ethico-theological characterization as "heavenly realm" in Fichte 1962, I/16:136.
66 See Kant 1900, 6:93–147 (*Religion within the Bounds of Mere Reason*); Kant 1996a, 129–171.
67 See Fichte 1962, II/16:66–71.
68 See *Republic* 719 e-722 c; Plato 1961, 1310–1312.
69 *Republic* 473d; Plato 1985, 712f.
70 Fichte 1971, 7:612.

Appendix

1 Vgl. *Politeia* 332b–c; Plato 1985, 581.
2 See *Politeia* 332c–d, esp. 332d; Plato 1985, 581.
3 See *Politeia* 334b; Plato 1985, 583f.
4 See *Politeia* 353e; Plato 1985, 604.
5 See *Politeia* 368d–e; Plato 1985.
6 See *Politeia* 389b–c (not in bk. 2 but in bk. 3); Plato 1985, 634.
7 See *Politeia* 392a–b; Plato 1985, 637.
8 See *Politeia* 358c–362c (Glaucon) and 362c–367e (Glaucon's brother Adeimantos); Plato 1985, 606–609 and 609–614.
9 Note that in this translation square brackets indicate additions made by the translator.
10 See note 1.
11 See note 2.
12 See note 3.
13 See note 4.
14 See note 5.
15 See note 6.
16 See note 7.
17 See note 8.

Bibliography

Aristotle, 1985: The Complete Works. The Revised Oxford Translation. Ed. Jonathan Barnes. 2 vols. Princeton: Princeton University Press.

———, 1998: Politics. Transl. Ernest Baker. Rev. and introd. R. F. Stanley. Oxford: Oxford University Press.

Avineri, Shlomo, 1972: Hegel's Theory of the Modern State. Cambridge: Cambridge University Press.

Baron, Hans, 1955: The Crisis of the Early Italian Renaissance. Civic Humanism and Republican Liberty in an Age of Classicism and Tyranny. Princeton: Princeton University Press.

Conklin, William E., 2008: Hegel's Laws. The Legitimacy of a Modern Legal Order. Stanford: Stanford University Press.

Cummins, Phillip and Günter Zöller (Eds.), 1993: Minds, Ideas, and Objects. Essays on the Theory of Representation in Modern Philosophy. North American Kant Society Studies in Philosophy. Atascadero: Ridgeview.

Dickey, Laurence, 1987: Hegel. Religion, Economics, and the Politics of Spirit, 1770–1807. Cambridge: Cambridge University Press.

Döring, Tobias, Barbara Vinken, and Günter Zöller (Eds.), 2010: Übertragene Anfänge. Imperiale Figurationen um 1800. Munich: Wilhelm Fink.

Everdell, William R., 2000: The End of Kings. A History of Republics and Republicans. Chicago: University of Chicago Press.

Fichte, Johann Gottlieb, 1962: Gesamtausgabe der Bayerischen Akademie der Wissenschaften. Ed. Reinhard Lauth, Hans Gliwitzky, Hans Jacob, Erich Fuchs, Peter K. Schneider and Günter Zöller. Stuttgart-Bad Cannstatt: Fromann-Holzboog.

———, 1971: Werke. Ed. Immanuel Hermann Fichte. 11 vols. Berlin: De Gruyter. Original edition 1834–1835 and 1845–1846.

———, 1982. The Science of Knowledge with the First and Second Introductions. Transl. and ed. Peter Heath and John Lachs. Cambridge: Cambridge University Press.

———, 1988. Early Writings. Transl. and ed. Daniel Breazeale. Ithaca: Cornell University Press.

———, 1994. Introductions to the Wissenschaftslehre and Other Writings (1797–1800). Transl. and ed. Daniel Breazeale. Indianapolis: Hackett.

———, 1999: The Popular Works. Introd. Daniel Breazeale. 2 vols. London: Thoemmes. Reprinted from an edition of 1889.

———, 2000: Foundations of Natural Law According to the Wissenschaftslehre. Ed. Frederick Neuhouser. Transl. Michael Baur. Cambridge: Cambridge University Press.

———, 2005: The System of Ethics According to the Principles of the Wissenschaftslehre. Transl. and ed. Daniel Breazeale and Günter Zöller. Cambridge: Cambridge University Press.

———, 2012: The Closed Commercial State. Transl. Anthony Curtis Adler. Albany: State University of New York Press.

Goethe, Johann Wolfgang, 1994: Tages- und Jahreshefte. Sämtliche Werke, Briefe, Tagebücher und Gespräche. 40 in 45 vols. Series I, vol. 17. Ed. Imtraut Schmid. Frankfurt: Deutscher Klassiker Verlag.

Guillois, Antoine, 1889: Napoléon. L'homme, le politique, l'orateur, d'après sa correspondence et ses œuvres. 2 vols. Paris: Perrin et cie.

Gwynn, David M., 2012: The Roman Republic. A Very Short Introduction. Oxford: Oxford University Press.

Hahm, David E., 2009: The Mixed Constitution in Greek Thought. In: Ryan K. Balot (Ed.): A Companion to Greek and Roman Political Thought. Oxford: Wiley-Blackwell, 178–198.

Hegel, Georg Wilhelm Friedrich, 1968: Lectures on the History of Philosophy. 3 vols. Transl. E. S. Haldane and Frances H. Simson. London: Routledge and Paul.

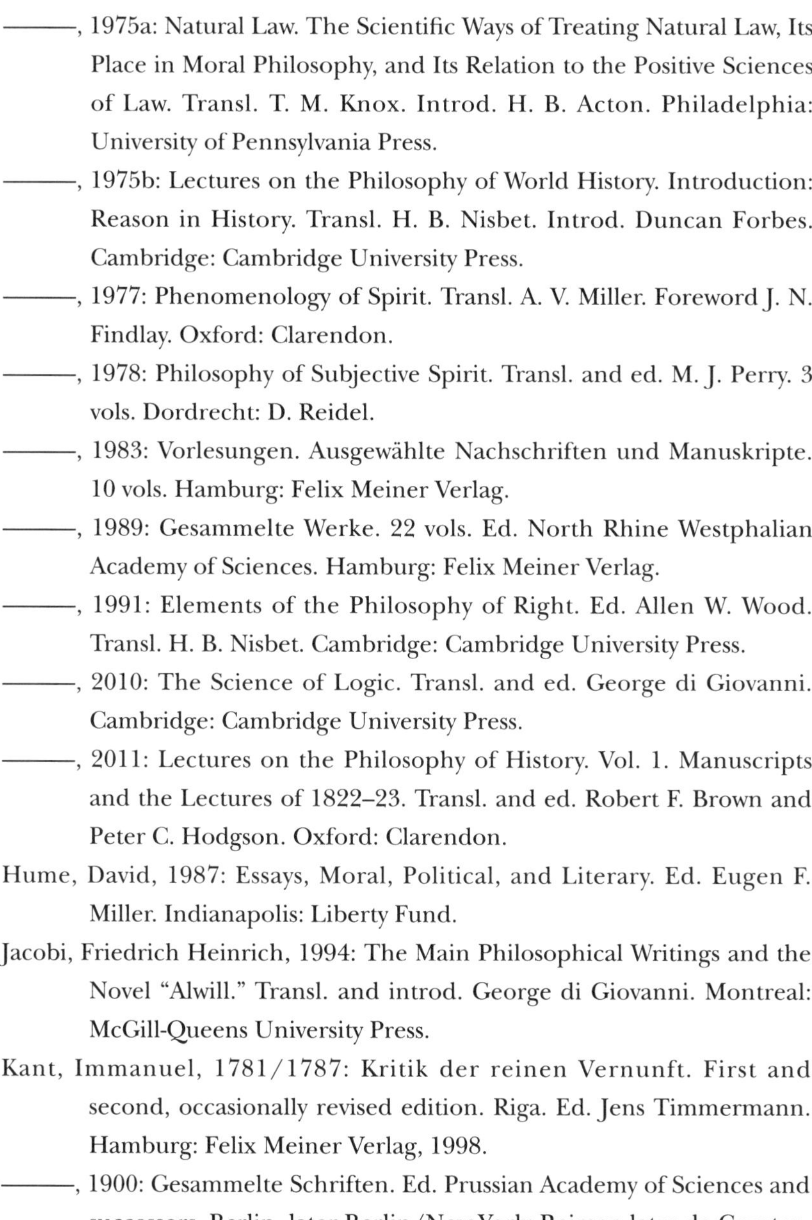

———, 1975a: Natural Law. The Scientific Ways of Treating Natural Law, Its Place in Moral Philosophy, and Its Relation to the Positive Sciences of Law. Transl. T. M. Knox. Introd. H. B. Acton. Philadelphia: University of Pennsylvania Press.

———, 1975b: Lectures on the Philosophy of World History. Introduction: Reason in History. Transl. H. B. Nisbet. Introd. Duncan Forbes. Cambridge: Cambridge University Press.

———, 1977: Phenomenology of Spirit. Transl. A. V. Miller. Foreword J. N. Findlay. Oxford: Clarendon.

———, 1978: Philosophy of Subjective Spirit. Transl. and ed. M. J. Perry. 3 vols. Dordrecht: D. Reidel.

———, 1983: Vorlesungen. Ausgewählte Nachschriften und Manuskripte. 10 vols. Hamburg: Felix Meiner Verlag.

———, 1989: Gesammelte Werke. 22 vols. Ed. North Rhine Westphalian Academy of Sciences. Hamburg: Felix Meiner Verlag.

———, 1991: Elements of the Philosophy of Right. Ed. Allen W. Wood. Transl. H. B. Nisbet. Cambridge: Cambridge University Press.

———, 2010: The Science of Logic. Transl. and ed. George di Giovanni. Cambridge: Cambridge University Press.

———, 2011: Lectures on the Philosophy of History. Vol. 1. Manuscripts and the Lectures of 1822–23. Transl. and ed. Robert F. Brown and Peter C. Hodgson. Oxford: Clarendon.

Hume, David, 1987: Essays, Moral, Political, and Literary. Ed. Eugen F. Miller. Indianapolis: Liberty Fund.

Jacobi, Friedrich Heinrich, 1994: The Main Philosophical Writings and the Novel "Alwill." Transl. and introd. George di Giovanni. Montreal: McGill-Queens University Press.

Kant, Immanuel, 1781/1787: Kritik der reinen Vernunft. First and second, occasionally revised edition. Riga. Ed. Jens Timmermann. Hamburg: Felix Meiner Verlag, 1998.

———, 1900: Gesammelte Schriften. Ed. Prussian Academy of Sciences and successors. Berlin, later Berlin/New York: Reimer, later de Gruyter.

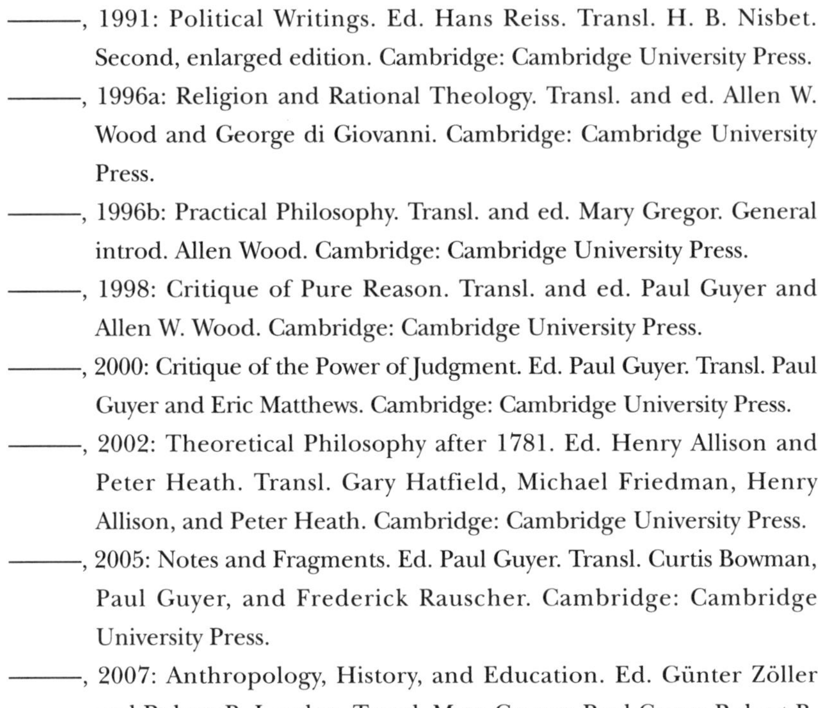

———, 1991: Political Writings. Ed. Hans Reiss. Transl. H. B. Nisbet. Second, enlarged edition. Cambridge: Cambridge University Press.

———, 1996a: Religion and Rational Theology. Transl. and ed. Allen W. Wood and George di Giovanni. Cambridge: Cambridge University Press.

———, 1996b: Practical Philosophy. Transl. and ed. Mary Gregor. General introd. Allen Wood. Cambridge: Cambridge University Press.

———, 1998: Critique of Pure Reason. Transl. and ed. Paul Guyer and Allen W. Wood. Cambridge: Cambridge University Press.

———, 2000: Critique of the Power of Judgment. Ed. Paul Guyer. Transl. Paul Guyer and Eric Matthews. Cambridge: Cambridge University Press.

———, 2002: Theoretical Philosophy after 1781. Ed. Henry Allison and Peter Heath. Transl. Gary Hatfield, Michael Friedman, Henry Allison, and Peter Heath. Cambridge: Cambridge University Press.

———, 2005: Notes and Fragments. Ed. Paul Guyer. Transl. Curtis Bowman, Paul Guyer, and Frederick Rauscher. Cambridge: Cambridge University Press.

———, 2007: Anthropology, History, and Education. Ed. Günter Zöller and Robert B. Louden. Transl. Mary Gregor, Paul Guyer, Robert B. Louden, Holly Wilson, Allen W. Wood, Günter Zöller, and Arnulf Zweig. Cambridge: Cambridge University Press.

Marx, Karl, 1970: Critique of Hegel's "Philosophy of Right." Transl. Annette Jolin and Joseph O'Malley. Ed. Joseph O'Malley. Cambridge: Cambridge University Press.

Münkler, Herfried, 2002: Republik, Demokratie und Diktatur. Die Rezeption von drei antiken Begriffen im politischen Denken der Neuzeit. In: Walter Jens and Bernd Seidensticker (Eds.): Ferne und Nähe der Antike. Berlin: De Gruyter, 69–98.

Natorp, Paul, 1903: Platos Ideenlehre. Eine Einführung in den Idealismus. Leipzig. Reprint, Hamburg: Felix Meiner Verlag, 2004.

Nelson, E., 2004: The Greek Tradition in Republican Thought. Cambridge: Cambridge University Press.

———, 2010: The Hebrew Republic. Jewish Sources and the Transformation of European Political Thought. Cambridge, Mass.: Harvard University Press.

Patten, Alan, 1999: Hegel's Idea of Freedom. Oxford: Oxford University Press.

Pettit, Philip, 1997: Republicanism. A Theory of Freedom and Government. Oxford: Oxford University Press.

Piché, Claude, 2003: La Doctrine de L'Etat de 1813 et la question de l'éducation chez Fichte. In: Jean-Christophe Goddard and Marc Maesschalck (Eds.): Fichte. La philosophie de la maturité (1804–1814). Reflexivité, phénoménologie et philosophie. Paris: Vrin, 159–174.

Plato, 1985: The Collected Dialogues of Plato Including the Letters. Ed. Edith Hamilton and Huntington Cairns. Princeton: Princeton University Press.

Pocock, J. G. A., 1975: The Machiavellian Moment. Florentine Political Thought and the Atlantic Republican Tradition. Princeton: Princeton University Press.

———, 2010: Machiavelli and Rome. The Republic as Ideal and as History. In: John M. Najemy (Ed.): The Cambridge Companion to Machiavelli. Cambridge: Cambridge University Press, 144–156.

Popper, Karl R., 1945: The Open Society and Its Enemies. Vol. 1: The Spell of Plato. London: Routledge.

Rahe, Paul A., 1992: Republics Ancient and Modern. Classical Republicanism and the American Revolution. 2 vols. Chapel Hill: University of North Carolina Press.

Rametta, Gaetano, 2003: Doctrine de la science et Doctrine de L'Etat. La dissolution de la théologie politique chez le dernier Fichte. In: Jean-Christophe Goddard and Marc Maesschalck (Eds.): Fichte. La philosophie de la maturité (1804–1814). Reflexivité, phénoménologie et philosophie. Paris: Vrin, 143–158.

Reich, Klaus, 1935: Kant und die Ethik der Griechen. Tübingen: J. C. B. Mohr [Paul Siebeck].

Santozki, Ulrike, 2006: Die Bedeutung antiker Theorien für die Genese und Systematik von Kants Philosophie. Eine Analyse der drei Kritiken. Berlin: De Gruyter.

Sieyès, Emmanuel Joseph, 2003: Political Writings. Including the Debate between Sieyès and Tom Paine in 1791. Ed. Michael Sonenscher. Indianapolis: Hackett.

Skinner, Quentin, 2012: Liberty Before Liberalism. Cambridge: Cambridge University Press. First published 1998.

Taylor, Charles, 1979: Hegel and the Modern State. Cambridge: Cambridge University Press.

Thucydides, 1996: The Landmark Thucydides. A Companion Guide to the Peloponnesian War. Ed. Robert D. Strassler. Introd. Victor D. Hanson. New York: Free Press.

Tocqueville, Alexis de, 2000: Democracy in America. Transl. Harvey C. Mansfield and Delba Winthrop. Chicago: University of Chicago Press.

Wundt, Max, 1929: Fichte-Forschungen. 2nd edition. Stuttgart-Bad Cannstatt: Friedrich Frommann Verlag, 1976.

Zöller, Günter, 1998: Fichte's Transcendental Philosophy. The Original Duplicity of Intelligence and Will. Cambridge: Cambridge University Press. Cambridge Paperback Edition, 2002.

———, 2003b: "Das Absolute und seine Erscheinung: Die Schelling-Rezeption des späten Fichte." In Internationales Jahrbuch des deutschen Idealismus/International Yearbook of German Idealism 1, 165–182.

———, 2003c: "Pax Kantiana: Kant e la pace perpetua in filosofia." In: Gaetano Rametta (Ed.): Filosofia e guerra nell'età dell'idealismo Tedesco. Milan: Franco Angeli, 51–64.

———, 2008: "Politische Hermeneutik. Die philosophische Auslegung der Geschichte in Fichtes Reden an die deutsche Nation." In: Günter Figal (Ed.): Internationales Jahrbuch für Hermeneutik. Vol. 7. "Hermeneutik der Geschichte." Tübingen: Möhr-Siebeck Verlag, 219–243.

———, 2009: " 'Menschenbildung.' Staatspolitische Erziehung beim späten Fichte." In: Axel Hutter/Markus Kartheiniger (Eds.): Bildung als Mittel und Selbstzweck. Korrektive Erinnerung wider die Verengung des Bildungsbegriffs. Freiburg i. Br./Munich: Alber, 42-62.

——— (Ed.), 2011a: Der Staat als Mittel zum Zweck: Fichte über Freiheit, Recht und Gesetz. Baden-Baden: Nomos Verlag.

———, 2011b: "Kant's Political Anthropology." In: Dietmar Heidemann (Ed.): Kant Yearbook. Vol. 3. Berlin: De Gruyter, 131–161.

———, 2011c: "Der negative und der positive Nutzen der Ideen: Kant über die Grenzbestimmung der reinen Vernunft." In: Bernd Dörflinger and Günter Kruck (Eds.): Über den Nutzen von Illusionen. Die regulativen Ideen in Kants theoretischer Philosophie. Hildesheim: Georg Olms Verlag, 13–27.

———, 2011d: "Die beiden Grundprincipien der Menschheit: Glaube und Verstand in Fichtes später Staatsphilosophie." In: Jens Halfwassen, Markus Gabriel, and Stephan Zimmermann (Eds.): Philosophie und Religion. Heidelberg: Universitätsverlag Winter Heidelberg, 171–191.

———, 2013a: "Reflexion und Regulation: Kant über Begriffe und Prinzipien der Vernunft in der Kritik der Urteilskraft." In: Bernd Dörflinger and Günter Kruck (Eds.): Worauf die Philosophie hinaussieht: Kants regulative Ideen im Kontext von Teleologie und praktischer Philosophie. Hildesheim: Georg Olms Verlag, 31–48.

———, 2013b: Fichte lesen. Stuttgart-Bad Cannstatt: Frommann-Holzboog.

———, 2014a: "Homo homini civis: The Modernity of Classical German Political Philosophy." Forthcoming in: Anders Moe Rasmussen (Ed.): German Idealism Today. Berlin and Boston: De Gruyter.

———, 2014b: "Between Rousseau and Freud. Kant on Cultural Uneasiness." In: Oliver Thorndike (Ed.): Rethinking Kant. vol. 3. Newcastle upon Tyne: Cambridge Scholars, 52-77.

———, 2014c: "Fichte (1762-1814)." Forthcoming in: Michael N. Forster and Kristin Gjesdal (Eds.): Oxford Handbook to German 19th Century Philosophy. Oxford: Oxford University Press.

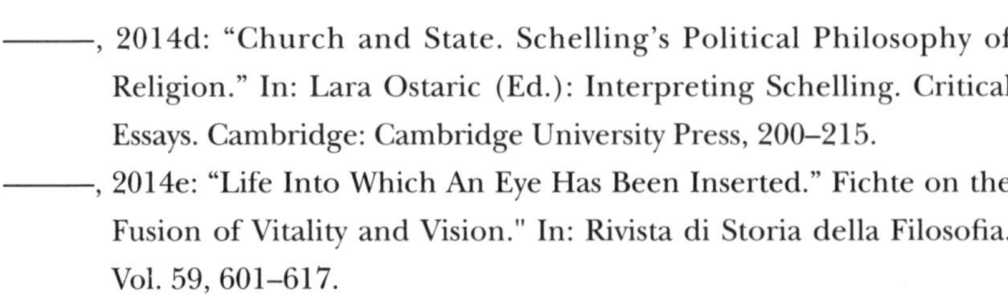

———, 2014d: “Church and State. Schelling’s Political Philosophy of Religion.” In: Lara Ostaric (Ed.): Interpreting Schelling. Critical Essays. Cambridge: Cambridge University Press, 200–215.

———, 2014e: “Life Into Which An Eye Has Been Inserted.” Fichte on the Fusion of Vitality and Vision." In: Rivista di Storia della Filosofia. Vol. 59, 601–617.